Biblical Thinking for Bu

M000232630

IX 9Marks Journal

info@9marks.org | www.9marks.org

Tools like this are provided by the generous investment of donors.
Each gift to 9Marks helps equip church leaders with a biblical vision and practical
resources for displaying God's glory to the nations through healthy churches.

Donate at: www.9marks.org/donate.

Or make checks payable to "9Marks" and mail to:
9 Marks
525 A St. NE
Washington, DC 20002

Editorial Director: Jonathan Leeman
Editor: Sam Emadi
Managing Editor: Alex Duke
Layout: Rubner Durais
Cover Design: OpenBox9
Production Manager: Rick Denham & Mary Beth Freeman
9Marks President: Mark Dever
Paperback ISBN: 978-1-951474-76-8
eBook ISBN: 978-1-951474-77-5

BUILDING UP YOUR PASTORS

BUILDING UP BY REACHING OUT

Editor's Note

Jonathan Leeman

For years now, 9Marks has argued that church membership is not just a status, it's a job. By joining a church, you're not joining a club, you're stepping into an office. Jesus has given you work to do, and he's given you the competence and authority to do it.

Most 9Marks Journals aim at pastors and church leaders. This one was written for members. Its purpose is to lay out some of the essential elements of that job. So we called it a guidebook. Print it out. Read it one article at a time over a month. Ask God how you might better serve your fellow members, your pastors, and your non-Christian neighbors.

Many other things in the news and the culture wars might be grabbing your attention right now. But amidst all that, don't forget to spend time with your kids, be a good neighbor, work hard for your employer, and—our point here—work to build up your church. Aside from caring for your family, it might be the most important thing you can do to *make a difference* in the world around you, to say nothing of doing eternal good in people's lives.

So, church member, here is the job you have to do. We pray it encourages you to grow in love for and service to Christ's bride.

Be Like Batman: Guard the Gospel

Sam Emadi

atman is a model church member.

    I bet you never thought you'd read that sentence in a 9Marks article, huh? But think about it for a moment. Batman's just an ordinary person, a regular guy roaming the streets of Gotham in a batsuit bringing justice to criminals. He doesn't have special Kryptonian DNA like Superman. He was never injected with a super soldier serum like Captain America. But when the Dark Knight sees the bat symbol light up the sky, he suits up and gets to work *guarding* the city of Gotham. He's an ordinary man with an extraordinary task.

What does any of this have to do with your role as a church member? Well, quite a bit. Church members have been commissioned by God to *guard the gospel.* That task may seem like something that should be entrusted to spiritual superheroes. But God in his wisdom has put that responsibility on every Christian as a member of a local church.

Let's see this in the Bible.

GUARDING GOD'S DWELLING

The story of redemption actually begins with God commissioning Adam to "guard" the Garden of Eden, the dwelling place of God (Gen

2:15). As creation's priest-king, Adam had the responsibility to protect Eden from sin's defiling influence. When the serpent slithered into the garden and began tempting his wife, Adam shirked his responsibility. The bat-symbol flashed in the sky, but Adam refused to suit up. Instead, he passively followed his wife into disobedience (Gen 3:6).

But thankfully, the story didn't end there. A better priest-king, the Lord Jesus, came to earth to defeat the Serpent and succeed where Adam failed. In so doing, Jesus created a new kingdom of priests and commissioned them, like Adam, to guard God's new dwelling place on earth, the local church (1 Cor. 3:16–17; 1 Pet. 2:9).

We see this point most clearly in Matthew 16 and Matthew 18. In Matthew 16, Jesus asks the apostles who they think he is. Peter pipes up first: "You are the Christ, the Son of the living God." Jesus' reply is a stunning statement not just about Peter but about all those who imitate Peter's faith:

And Jesus answered him, "Blessed are you, Simon Bar-Jonah! For flesh and blood has not revealed this to you, but my Father who is in heaven. And I tell you, you are Peter, and on this rock I will build my church, and the gates of hell shall not prevail against it. I will give you the keys of the kingdom of heaven, and whatever you bind on earth shall be bound in heaven, and whatever you loose on earth shall be loosed in heaven." (Matt. 16:17–19)

Jesus is going to build his church on Peter—the confessor and his confession. But more than that, Jesus is going to give Peter and the other apostles the "keys of the kingdom of heaven," such that they, like Jesus, declare confessions of faith as from heaven.

Perhaps even more remarkable, however, is that Jesus gives this same authority ("the keys of the kingdom of heaven") not just to the apostles, but to local churches of ordinary men and women who believe in Jesus.

If your brother sins against you, go and tell him his fault, between you and him alone. If he listens to you, you have gained your brother. But if he does not listen, take one or two others along with you, that every charge may be established by the evidence of two or three witnesses. If he refuses to listen to them, tell it to the church. And if he refuses to listen even to the church, let him be to you as a Gentile and a tax collector. Truly, I say to you, whatever you bind on earth shall be bound in heaven, and whatever you loose on earth shall be loosed in heaven. Again I say to you, if two of you agree on earth about anything they ask, it will be done for them by my Father in heaven. For where two or three are gathered in my name, there am I among them." (Matt. 18:15–20).

In Matthew 18, we see that local churches (the members, not just the leadership) must guard the gospel by overseeing one another's membership in the kingdom of God. They do that by overseeing a person's *life* and their *confession* to ensure that it's consistent with the gospel. Each church member must *guard the gospel* both in their life and in the lives of fellow church members.

HOW EXACTLY DO WE DO THIS?

OK, so church members must guard the gospel. We're priest-kings commissioned to carry out this task. But how exactly do we do this?

Well, the answer requires more than enumerating a to-do list. Instead, we need to recognize that every aspect of the Christian life should contribute to this overarching commission.

- We affirm others as fellow church members by baptism and the Lord's Supper when we recognize the gospel in their life and in their confession.
- We disciple others as a way of guarding the purity of the gospel in their lives.
- We ask others to disciple us to ensure that we contribute to the church's health and can faithfully carry out our responsibilities as priest-kings in the kingdom of God.
- We bar from communion those who live out of accord with the gospel or confess a gospel contrary to Scripture.
- We clearly articulate our gospel profession by affirming a biblical statement of faith.
- We expel false teachers from our midst, even firing them

from the church if their message is inconsistent with the gospel (Gal 1:8).

- We submit to godly elders who lead the church in knowing how best to guard the gospel.

In all of these ways and more, we guard the gospel.

ORDINARY PEOPLE WITH AN EXTRAORDINARY TASK

Each Lord's Day, God's people gather to sit under the preaching of God's Word. Faithful preaching is like igniting the bat-symbol. God's Word shines a light in the sky and calls God's people to action. They hear the message of the gospel and their responsibility to guard that gospel in their own lives and in the life of their local congregation.

Then they get to work.

One brother confesses his indulgence in pornography to another and asks for help and accountability. A sister asks another for forgiveness for gossiping about her. An older man in the congregation asks a new Christian to meet each week so they can read Romans together. A husband and wife extend hospitality to lonely, isolated members. Another brother confronts a man who's refusing to turn from his gambling addiction.

Each act in its own way protects the gospel. Each member of the body plays a part. Each ordinary Christian carries out an extraordinary task.

Friend, if you're a member of a church, do you realize that this is your job too? You don't need a seminary education. You don't have to be an ordained minister or a spiritual superstar. All you need is the Holy Spirit, and you have that! It's time to suit up and start guarding the gospel.

ABOUT THE AUTHOR

Sam Emadi is a member of Third Avenue Baptist Church in Louisville, KY and serves as the Senior Editor at 9Marks.

Show Up!

Mike Gilbart-Smith

F olks attending the membership class at our church are often surprised at the emphasis we place on attending our Lord's Day gathering. However gifted someone might be at talking to teenagers or working on the website, we insist their presence at corporate worship is a far more essential and significant way to serve the flock. This priority isn't just a particular quirk of *our* church; it should be a biblical priority for *every* church.

Let's look at four reasons the Bible prioritizes gathering, followed by four ways that gathering is currently under threat.

FOUR REASONS THE BIBLE PRIORITIZES GATHERING

1) The presence of the Lord commends it.

The Lord Jesus promises his presence at the gathering of his people: "Where two or three are gathered in my name, there am I with them" (Matt. 18:20).

In light of the whole biblical narrative, this passage shows the extraordinary eschatological implications of the gathering. God's presence was lost in Eden (Gen 3:8), but it returned in some capacity in the tabernacle (Exod. 25:8, 22), the land (Num. 35:34), and the temple (1 Kgs. 8:10–11). But his presence with Israel was always limited: "Will God indeed dwell on the earth?" (1 Kgs. 8:27).

In the coming of Christ, God came to dwell with and die for his people (John 1:14; 10:11–15) so that those who receive the Son might become the gathered children of God (John 1:11–13; 11:51–52). And now, since the risen Christ is present among his gathered people, we have the privilege of joining with him as his brothers and sisters, praising his Father and ours (cf. Ps. 22:22; Heb. 2:12).

The very word that Jesus chooses for his community, *ekklesia,* implies that the church is "a society of men called out of some place or state and congregated in an assembly." [1] We are still the church during the week as we are scattered, but we are only the church during the week because we gather on the Lord's Day.

Our present, earthbound gatherings anticipate the time when he will dwell with us visibly (Rev. 21:3; 22:4). What a privilege and a promise! Who would want to miss out on that?

2) The command of the Lord requires it.

Gathering isn't just a privilege, it's also a command that creates a solemn responsibility. "Do not give

[1] Francis Turretin, *Institutes of Elenctic Theology Volume 3* (Phillipsburg, PA: P&R, 1997), 6.

up meeting together, as some are in the habit of doing, but encourage one another—and all the more as you see the Day approaching" (Heb. 10:25).

Throughout the New Testament, we see the weekly gathering of the church on the Lord's day as both a pattern and a precept (1 Cor. 5:4, Luke 24:33 John 20:19, Acts 20:7, 1 Cor. 16:2).

3) The community of the Lord needs it.

Gathering is commended and commanded for our good. One of the primary purposes of gathering together is mutual edification. True, the church can be built up through informal and small group conversations during the week. But the New Testament repeatedly emphasizes that the church is edified when it "comes together" (1 Cor. 11:20, 33, 34; 14:26).

4) The pictures of church imply it.

The images Scripture uses to describe the church highlight the necessity of gathering. The church is the body of Christ that recognises the other parts of the body particularly as they gather together as one body

(Rom. 12:3–8, 1 Cor. 10:17, 11:29, 12:12–31, 14:1–19). The church is a temple where all the stones are built together through the mutual edification that occurs as they gather (1 Cor. 3:16–17, Eph. 2:19–22). The church is a family where we feed one another with the Word of God (Col. 3:16) around the table of the Lord. The church is a flock of sheep that are together in the sheepfold.

FOUR CONTEMPORARY THREATS TO THE CORPORATE GATHERING

1) "Virtual meetings" are convenient.

The past year has highlighted for some that virtual meetings seem safer and more convenient than real meetings. Certainly, the pandemic posed some legitimate reasons for temporarily abstaining from assembling. But it should never set an enduring precedent.

2) Inadequate meetings make us cynical.

Finding a healthy church can be hard. But the prevalence of unhealthy churches should motivate us to find and join a healthy church. It shouldn't cause us to retreat into a churchless Christianity.

Our private devotion ought to complement and supplement the gathering of the church. It should never compensate for its absence or supplant it entirely.

3) We concentrate on friendship elsewhere.

Pastors commonly notice that members sometimes attend church infrequently because they're visiting other churches—perhaps rubbing shoulders with friends and family.

Of course, it's not wrong to visit friends in other churches. But we harm the body when these visits are frequent rather than occasional.

Additionally, social media has made it easier to feel continually connected to those who live at a distance. But when our wider friendships diminish our ability to grow together with our local church family, we are spreading ourselves too thin, and the life of the local body will become shallower.

4) We spend our time with non-Christians.

Opportunities to build new relationships with those who don't know Christ are precious and sometimes difficult. As a result, some suggest that for the sake of mission Christians should prioritize spending time with non-Christians over time with their local church. Sure, the church gathering might build you and other believers up. But you're already saved! So why party in the lifeboat while others are drowning? Furthermore, in a post-Christian society, fewer and fewer of those souls would ever darken the doors of a church.

I love the evangelistic zeal behind such an appeal. But I fear it's short-sighted and self-defeating. How will the congregation be equipped and motivated to reach the lost without a weekly, glory-anticipating gathering? How will all people know that we are Jesus' disciples if our love for the lost is greater than our love for one another (Jn. 13:34–35)?

CHRISTIAN, GATHER!

This last year the Lord, in his sovereign goodness, removed from many of us the ability to gather regularly for worship, edification, and service. I pray that as we're able to gather once again, every member will return. Remote, virtual, disembodied fellowship simply isn't enough. We've made do with it. But hopefully it has caused us to value all the more the close, real, embodied gathering that anticipates how we will spend eternity—together in the presence of our Lord.

ABOUT THE AUTHOR

Mike Gilbart-Smith is the pastor of Twynholm Baptist Church in Fulham, England.

Contribute to the Needs of the Saints

Alex Hong

"**W**hat's taking so long?" my five-year-old whined, wandering into the dining room and slumping into a chair. My wife responded from the stove, "If you would like dinner to be ready more quickly, you can help set the table, or pour water into the cups, or help your little sisters wash their hands." Young children often expect things to be done according to their own timing and desires. When they're not served the way they want to be served, they often throw a temper tantrum.

Sadly, sometimes Christians act like young children. They expect things to get done for them instead of finding opportunities to serve their church family. If the songs don't fit their musical taste, or if the preaching doesn't build them up, or if the fellowship doesn't encourage them, they become overtly critical and eventually leave.

Don't get me wrong, a church should edify its members. But that doesn't mean it exists to serve the kingdom of Self.

Instead of thinking like a spiritual consumer, church members should think like spiritual contributors. I suspect that if every Christian saw themselves as contributors more than consumers, there would be fewer spiritual temper tantrums and more encouraging family gatherings.

God's Word tells us we ought to "contribute to the needs of the saints" (Rom. 12:13).

"CONTRIBUTING" MEANS MORE THAN GIVING, BUT NOT LESS THAN GIVING

The word "contribute" means more than just giving money. Commenting on Romans 12:13, Martyn Lloyd-Jones explains,

Paul is saying that you do not merely distribute to the necessities of the saints, but that you enter into fellowship with them; you become partners with them; you share with them. In other words, you must feel that their burden is your burden, that you are in hardship with them, and that you really are feeling it yourself. You have entered into a kind of partnership with them in their predicament.[2]

Because we belong to one another (Rom. 12:4–5), Christians help each other because "if one member suffers, all suffer together" (1 Cor. 12:26). Paul isn't advocating general philanthropy, but exhorting

2 D. M. Lloyd Jones, *Romans: An Exposition of Chapter 12 Christian Conduct* (Carlisle, PA: Banner of Truth Trust, 2000), 409.

Christians to share with *the saints.* The "saints" are those who have been set apart by God and saved by his great transforming mercy in Christ (Rom. 12:1–2).

Paul exhorts believers to "do good to everyone, and *especially to those who are of the household of faith*" (Gal. 6:10). A tangible expression of our love for Christ is love for fellow believers in need (1 John 3:16–17). Amy Carmichael, the famous Christian missionary to India, once said, "You can give without loving, but you cannot love without giving." Because we belong to God and to one another, we *demonstrate* our love and belonging by contributing to family members when they are in need.

THE EARLY CHURCH'S EXAMPLE

The early church in Jerusalem modeled this virtue. Many first-century Christians were excluded from their families and persecuted by religious and secular authorities because of their faith. They often lacked basic necessities such as food, clothing, and shelter. So the church became their new family and met their basic needs.

They not only sold their possessions, but they *distributed* the proceeds to all as any had *need* (Acts 2:45). They "had everything in common" and shared their personal possessions because they "had a better possession and an abiding one" (Heb. 10:34). Luke tells us "there was not a needy person among them, for as many as were owners of land or houses sold them and brought the proceeds of what was sold and laid it at the apostle's feet, and"—again— "it was *distributed* to each as *any had need*" (Acts 4:32–35).

These early church members had compassion on their fellow believers. They had "favor with all the people" and "the Lord added to their number day by day those who were being saved" (Acts 2:47). The church's generosity became a powerful evangelistic witness.

MEETING FAMILY NEEDS

Contributing to the needs of the saints means more than just giving a sporadic Sunday offering. So what are some practical ways you can contribute to the saints' needs?

Join a local church.

It becomes exceedingly more difficult to contribute to the needs of the saints if you are an anonymous Christian. You need to join a healthy local church where the gospel is preached and the sacraments are properly administered. By joining a local church, you commit yourself to loving real people who aren't like you and whom you otherwise would never have known.

Commit to regularly attending church.

You cannot contribute to the needs of saints you don't know and never see. One reason of many to regularly gather with your church is to be spurred on to specific opportunities to love others through good works (Heb. 10:24–25). So commit to attending the Sunday gatherings of your church. Commit to members' meetings, prayer meetings, Bible studies, and small group. The more you're involved, the more you'll discover the opportunities that exist to share your life and to meet real needs.

Pray for the members of your church.

As you faithfully attend the family gatherings of your church, the Lord will present opportunities to pray for people. If a church has a membership directory, pray regularly and systematically for other members. As you pray, the Lord will bring needs and opportunities to mind as you learn about various members' burdens and prayer requests.

Be faithful in your vocation.

Ephesians 4:28 says, "Let the thief no longer steal, but rather let him labor, doing honest work with his own hands, so that he may have something *to share with anyone in need.*" We get jobs and work hard so that we won't be a burden to others and so that we will be able to bless others with our resources.

Share your needs.

There will be times when you are in need. Family members can't help you if they don't know *your* needs. God has designed the church so that its members will carry each other's burdens (Gal. 6:2).

Prioritize giving to your church.

Deliberately put "something aside and store it up" as you prosper. And then give faithfully, proportionally, cheerfully, generously, and sacrificially (1 Cor. 16:2; 2 Cor. 8:1–5, 12; 9:6–7).

SUPPLYING THE NEEDS OF OTHERS

What happens when church members obey Paul's instructions to contribute to the needs of the saints? Paul says, "For the ministry of this service is not only supplying the needs of the saints but is also overflowing in many thanksgivings to God. By their approval of this service, they will glorify God because of your submission that comes from your confession of the gospel of Christ, and the generosity of your contribution for them and for all others" (2 Cor. 9:12–13).

In other words, when needs are met, thanksgiving abounds, obedience is manifested, the church is built up, and God is glorified!

When you contribute to the needs of the saints, you store up treasure for yourself as a good foundation for the future, so that you take hold of that which is truly life (1 Tim. 6:17–19). And we all long for that final day when our King will tell us, "Well done, good and faithful servant" (Matt. 25:23, 31–45).

ABOUT THE AUTHOR

Alex Hong is the Senior Pastor of Christian Fellowship Bible Church.

Sing to One Another

Matt Boswell

S ome of my earliest memories involve singing in church. I can still see my dad standing on the front row before he would get up to preach. He would bounce on his toes a bit while singing with a full voice and lifted eyebrows. I can still see my mom, perched in the choir loft with joy on her face. I remember older saints as they joined in the great hymns of our faith.

In short, congregational singing has played a formative role in my life both theologically and spiritually. The hymns we sang helped me both know and sing the truths we hold so dearly.

The Scriptures resound with singing. There are over fifty direct commands for us to sing, and singing is mentioned over 400 times in the Bible. Singing doesn't merely play a one-dimensional function in the life of the church; it plays a multi-faceted, invaluable role as we worship God. It shapes our discipleship, and declaration to the world.

Psalm 96:1–3 functions as a microcosm that helps us see this clearly. It highlights three reasons why we sing.

1. WE SING AS AN ACT OF WORSHIP.

Singing, first and foremost, is an act of worship to God. Psalm 96:1–2a stresses the importance of God being the first audience of our song.

"Oh sing to the LORD a new song; sing to the LORD, all the earth! Sing to the LORD, bless his name."

Notice the triple emphasis on the Lord. Don Carson defines worship as "the proper response of all moral, sentient beings to God, ascribing all honor and worth to their Creator-God precisely because he is worthy, delightfully so." In this definition, we see a connection between blessing the Lord and singing. When Christians sing to God—whether alone, with our family, or at church—it's an act of delightful worship.

2. WE SING TO DISCIPLE ONE ANOTHER.

To use the language of Psalm 96:2, as we sing, we should "tell his salvation from day to day." Notice the content of this song: the salvation of God.

The good news of the gospel builds us up, so we should sing to each other about it. That's how we help one another grow as Christians. Paul communicates this idea in his letter to the Colossians: "Let the word of Christ dwell in you richly, teaching and admonishing one another in all wisdom, singing psalms and hymns and spiritual songs, with thankfulness in your hearts to God" (Col. 3:16). Paul highlights for us that singing is a means of disciple-making.

3. WE SING AS A DECLARATION TO THE WORLD.

Consider Psalm 96:3: "Declare his glory among the nations, his marvelous works among all the peoples!" The hymns we sing as a church should be saturated with the marvelous works of God. They're little messengers of the truths we believe; we sing them to unconverted friends. Our act of singing is also a wonderful declaration to the world of our unity in Christ. John 13:35 says the world will know we are Christians by our love. So our act of congregational singing is itself an apologetic to an onlooking world of our shared salvation.

On this next Lord's Day, I hope you will sing from the bottom of your heart with gratitude to the Lord as an act of worship. I pray that you will sing to your brothers and sisters in Christ as you lend your voice to building one another up as disciples. I pray that as we sing, the Lord would bring into our gatherings people to whom we can boldly declare the salvation of our God.

ABOUT THE AUTHOR

Matt Boswell is pastor of ministries and worship at Providence Church in Frisco, Texas.

Protect Sound Doctrine

Jaime Owens

Dear Church Members,

When my eyes fall on the Third Epistle of John, my heart swells, particularly when I come to that bit about walking. John writes to his friend Gaius: "I have no greater joy than to hear that my children are walking in the truth." Is there any greater joy for a pastor than to hear that those whom he's labored for and loved with the truth are walking in it?

It may seem to many of us a simple task, walking. But walking *in the truth*? That's a hazardous business. Christians don't walk along sun-blanketed beaches with crystalline ocean at our feet. We walk through mine fields until we make our way home. The dangers, in this war of words, aren't seen with the eye but heard with the ear. We might describe it as a Cold War against the truth. The dangers, spiritually speaking, are nothing short of nuclear.

WHAT IS SOUND DOCTRINE?

I'm writing to you, beloved, to reflect on how we can walk together more safely to our heavenly home. But how can we walk in the truth when it's taking fire from every direction? How can we shield the gospel in all its brilliant simplicity and convicting power? By protecting sound doctrine.

But what is sound doctrine? It's not the stuff of dry academics or the speculations of armchair theologians. Sound doctrine is teaching from God's Word that's faithful to God's Word! It's as rich and practical as the Bible because sound doctrine, simply put, is biblical preaching, teaching, and instruction. We might say that if God's Word is the heart of the church, sound doctrine is the blood pumping out from it, bringing life to the whole body.

HOW TO PROTECT SOUND DOCTRINE

So, how can we protect sound doctrine? First and foremost, by filling our church with it. God's truth is never as vulnerable as when it's rarely received.

For us, the danger isn't that the Word will go unpreached; rather, it's that we'll fail to put it first. We should ask ourselves a couple of questions: Is hearing God's Word among the things in my life that *must* be done? Or do I crowd it out of my schedule for more important things?

When hearing sound doctrine is optional, we'll hear it less. And the less we hear the truth, the more easily it will be twisted and exposed to distortion in our minds. One of my prayers is that we would be so committed to hearing sound doctrine, that when the Word is preached and taught among us, we would make every effort to show up because our greatest desire is to hear God speak to us so that we might walk in his ways.

But is protecting sound doctrine simply a matter showing up? Should we entrust this most important duty, to protect sound doctrine, to me, your pastor? Yes and no. You've called me in faith to serve you with the Word, and one of the reasons you've called me is because you believe that I live and preach sound doctrine. But surely, this responsibility is too weighty for one man.

One way for us to protect sound doctrine is to develop a culture of identifying those who rightly handle God's Word and raising them up as elders so that they might share in the faithful instruction of sound doctrine. A plurality of elders who watch over one another's lives and doctrine provide a valiant defense against unsound doctrine. By God's grace, we'll continue to develop this culture of vigilance.

Every church should care about their pastors' character and doctrine. However, the ultimate responsibility for sound doctrine and the overall health of our church doesn't fall on pastors alone, but on the entire membership of our church. It may be that the Apostle Paul knocked his Galatian hearers back in their chairs when he wrote: "But even if we or an angel from heaven should preach to you a gospel contrary to the one we preached to you, let him be accursed" (Gal. 1:8).

Who is a mere church member to call out their pastor? My friend, there's no such thing as a mere church member. The Lord has called you, along with your fellow members, to have ears so trained, so sensitive to God's Word, that you can discern between the truth and a lie. In this sacred duty, you're part sheep, part sheepdog. You're a member of the flock. But you're also its guardian. This may seem like more than you bargained for when you began considering membership at Tremont. But with so much at stake, I want to call you, as God's Word does, to be a sheepdog for the truth.

I also want to again invite you to share your thoughts with me about all that I preach and teach among the flock. I want to assure you that whether we agree or disagree, in the providence of God, I regard your questions and feedback to be tools that sharpen my understanding of God's Word and challenge me to pay closer attention. The dialogue between preacher and hearer must always be preserved, not only because it keeps the preacher accountable, but also because it's a channel for fruitful discussion about God's Word.

DOCTRINE ISN'T ENOUGH

Finally, churches may be filled with sound doctrine. From pastors to pew, we may guard orthodoxy with steely resolve. But if we don't apply sound doctrine to our lives and help each other do so, it's only a matter of time before the truth among us will be a casualty. We've seen the relics. Buildings that used to house churches that are now merely museums of past glory, if anything at all. At the end of the day, the only way that we will walk together safely home is if the sound doctrine we hear brings about a sound life. We need sound minds. We need steadfast hearts. More sound doctrine will not be enough. We need God's Spirit to make us sound. Pray that God would make us a sound church as we prize and protect sound doctrine.

Brothers and sisters, do you see how much of a part that you play in protecting sound doctrine? We're raging a truth war against the enemy. We're called to fight the good fight of faith, and to march forward in truth. It's hard but surely God, who's already given us the victory in Jesus Christ, will carry us when we can't walk. As John Newton once wrote and we now sing,

"Through many dangers, toils, and snares,
I have already come,
Tis' grace that brought me safe thus far
And Grace will lead me home."

By the grace of God, let's walk in the truth. For the feet of the One who walked before us were pieced for us. Surely, he will not leave us defenseless. Brothers and sisters, let's be faithful. Let's protect sound doctrine.

Walking out front and alongside of you, I am,

Your pastor,
Jaime

ABOUT THE AUTHOR

Jaime Owens is the senior pastor of Tremont Temple Baptist Church in Boston, Massachusetts.

Cleanse Out The Old Leaven

Matthias Lohmann

Beloved,

In recent times, we've all been very concerned about the spread of the coronavirus. But we should be even more concerned about the spread of sin. The Bible likens sin to leaven that spreads (Lk 12:1). Just a little bit of leaven has the potential to spoil a whole batch of dough (Gal 5:9; 1 Cor 5:6).

For this reason, the Apostle Paul writes to the church in Corinth: *"Cleanse out the old leaven that you may be a new lump, as you really are unleavened. For Christ, our Passover lamb, has been sacrificed"* (1 Cor 5:7). Let's consider this eternal truth so that we can apply it both corporately and individually.

CORPORATELY

As you know, we had to *"cleanse out the old leaven"* a few times in the past when we had to remove members from our church who continued in unrepentant sin. These were painful times for us—full of many tears and much pain. But we had to recognize that someone who had been part of our church body no longer gave clear evidence of being a Christian. As Paul writes, the church really is unleavened. If leaven is found in the church, it needs to be removed before it starts permeating the whole "batch of dough," the church. I'm grateful that we did have the courage to do what God's Word commanded.

Ultimately, cleansing out the old leaven is an act of love for all parties involved.

It's an act of love for the unbelievers who observe our church. By not accepting unrepentant sin in our midst, we showed ourselves as those who have indeed been called out of this world and made new in Christ.

It was also an act of love toward God, as we displayed a willingness to obey his Word even when it's painful. As Christ's body, we represent him, so allowing unrepentant sin would lie about his holiness.

It was also an act of love for the church at large. Acting otherwise would have allowed sin room to spread. This would have perhaps especially tempted younger Christians who may be deceived about sin and its destructive effects.

Finally, it was a display of love for the former member whom we disciplined. Why? Because we refused to let him or her be deceived over his or her own spiritual state. Every act of discipline ought to be done with the hope that it will lead to repentance and restoration: "that his spirit may be saved in the day of the Lord." (1 Cor 5:5). Indeed, as I write this, I recall how our Good Shepherd has used this tool to bring two formerly disciplined members back into our flock.

In all of this, we understand that "the leaven" we are removing are not necessarily people, but sin itself. Which helps us to see how the call to "cleanse out the old leaven" can also be applied to each of us individually.

INDIVIDUALLY

Dear brothers and sisters, if we are committed to root out sin corporately, we should also be committed to do this personally. The Bible calls us to pursue holiness and to fight sin (1 Thess 4:7); to be holy, as our God is holy (1 Pet 1:15). Indeed, Christians *are* holy. So let us be what we are. This is what Paul is calling us to when he writes: "Cleanse out the old leaven that you may be a new lump, as you really are unleavened."

Let's never assume that we can harbor a particular sin without it spreading—it will! Let's just look at a few examples. Pornography seems to many men as a small, rather harmless sin. But it won't take long until this leads to lies, and it promotes lustful thoughts that might lead to action. Or think about gossip. It seems like just a small comment about someone else. But once it spreads, it harms relationships. It promotes mistrust and leads to division in the church.

Therefore, we should be committed to cleansing out the leaven in our lives. Ultimately, we do this to honor our Lord who gave himself for us. That's precisely Paul's point: "Cleanse out the old leaven that you may be a new lump, as you really are unleavened. For Christ, our Passover lamb, has been sacrificed."

While this should motivate us to strive after holiness, it also encourages us when we fail. Because Christ, our Passover lamb, has been sacrificed, we can be assured of God's grace. Christ alone was free of any leaven—he was pure, blameless, and holy. And he took our sin so that we can stand before God even as we are still impure. And in him we have the power to battle sin until one day we will be transformed into his likeness.

So brothers and sisters, let's cleanse out the old leaven of sin both corporately through corrective church discipline and individually as we fight by grace the sin in our own lives.

ABOUT THE AUTHOR

Matthias Lohmann is the pastor of an evangelical church in downtown Munich, Germany, and one of the leaders of the German gospel partnership Evangelium21.

Prepare to Hear God's Word

9Marks

1. **Throughout the week, meditate on the passage that will be preached on Sunday.** Pray for your pastor as he prepares his sermon. Take notes on the text. Ask questions of the text. Pray through the text.

2. **Prepare for Sunday morning.** On Saturday night or Sunday morning, pray for your upcoming opportunity to hear God's Word preached. Pray that your heart would be soft and humble before it.

3. **Talk and pray about the sermon with friends after church.** Start conversations at lunch by asking, "How did the Scripture challenge or speak to you today?" Encourage others by sharing what you learned about God and his Word during the sermon. Talk to others about how you can specifically apply what you learned in the week ahead.

4. **Meditate and act on the sermon you heard throughout the week.** Don't let the Sunday sermon become a one-time event that fades from memory as soon as it is over (James 1:22-25). Review your sermon notes with friends or family. Choose one or two

applications from the Scripture and prayerfully put them into practice over the coming week.

EDITOR'S NOTE

Some of this material has been adapted from Thabiti Anyabwile's book *What is a Healthy Church Member?*, 22-25.

Be Hospitable

Doug Van Meter

When I saw the title of the book, I couldn't help but laugh: *Sorry, I'm Late, I Didn't Want to Come: An Introvert's Year of Living Dangerously.* I can relate. Connecting with people doesn't come easy for me. But I know that following Christ means being a part of a local church, and being a part of a local church means sometimes doing things that make you uncomfortable.

Hospitality isn't easy, but God requires it. So let me encourage you to "live dangerously" by showing hospitality.

THE BIBLE TELLS ME SO

The New Testament makes a big deal of hospitality. Did you realize that? Paul includes hospitality in the list of the basics of the Christian life (Rom. 12:13; also 1 Peter 4:9). He says our elders or pastors must be characterized by it (1 Tim. 3:2), presumably so that they can set an example for the congregation. He says it should also characterize the older women in the church (1 Tim. 5:10), presumably for the same reason.

Hospitality is not the responsibility of extroverts but of *every* church member.

Biblical hospitality means far more than cake and coffee after the evening service. Showing hospitality calls for an open home, an open schedule, an open ear, and even an open wallet. Here's my working definition of hospitality: *a Christ-driven, selfless willingness to sacrifice our goods for the good of others* (Rom. 12:13).

Christians must show hospitality to those we know, and to those we don't. Hebrews 13:2 makes this clear, "Do not neglect to show hospitality to strangers, for thereby some have entertained angels unawares." This passage clearly mandates that we show the sacrificial love of Christ to those outside our normal circle.

A stranger in Scripture isn't necessarily someone we're meeting for the first time. It may also refer to someone who is culturally different from us. In the Old Testament, a stranger was someone who was outside of God's covenant nation of Israel. Paul has this in mind when he writes that the Gentile converts in Ephesus had been "alienated from the commonwealth of Israel and strangers to the covenant of promise" (Eph. 2:12). Through the power of the gospel, they are now members of the household of God.

When it comes to hospitality, we must "pursue with zeal" the practical needs of others. We must show the love of Christ to those who are demographically different; to Christians from other churches who are passing through (see 3 John); to visitors who show up to our church; to new members who seem awkward; and to neighbors who seem strange!

So, young people should reach out to old people—and vice versa. Where I pastor (South Africa), this means white church members should seek meaningful connections with black church members—and vice versa. It means those of Afrikaans culture should open their doors to those of English culture.

LIKE OUR FATHER

Brothers and sisters, when we demonstrate practical love for the strangers and saints among us, we reflect our Heavenly Father. Jesus said, "For if you love those who love you, what reward do you have? . . . And if you greet only your brothers, what more are you doing than others?" (Matt. 5:46–47).

Our heavenly Father gave his Son in order to meet our greatest need, the forgiveness of our sins. He reconciled us to himself while we were strangers, strangers who were also enemies (Rom 5:8). As we reflect upon God's grace to us in Christ, our hearts ought to swell with a commitment to hospitality. We ought to reach out to others— without distinction— with sacrificial, needs-meeting love that leaves no room for grumbling (1 Pet. 4:9).

So Christians, whether you're an introvert or an extrovert, you're commanded to show hospitality even to the point of sacrifice—just like our Lord.

ABOUT THE AUTHOR

Doug Van Meter is the senior pastor of Brackenhurst Baptist Church in South Africa.

Disciple Others

Tony Shepherd

During eight years of pastoral ministry, few things have amazed me more than witnessing conversion. Seeing someone who was once spiritually dead come to life, turn away from their sin, and turn to Christ in faith—it's a wonder to behold! But another wonder I love to see is the gradual transformation of a believer as he or she becomes more like Jesus by the power of the Holy Spirit (2 Cor. 3:18).

This process of sanctification continues until we see Jesus face-to-face, and it's often spurred on by discipling relationships. Discipling is one of those words that gets thrown around a lot. But it simply means deliberately helping one another to grow in conformity to Jesus. Discipling is *deliberate* because it seeks to help *specific* individuals grow in *specific* ways toward godliness. Discipling is *mutual* because it's not a one-way street with a sage on one corner and a student on the other. Every Christian needs spiritual formation, and every Christian is equipped by the Spirit to build one another up (Jude 1:20; Eph. 4:12; 1 Peter 2:5). So discipling one another should be normal.

Now let's spend a little time thinking about the why, the who, and the how.

THE WHY?

I'll pick three reasons and elaborate on one.

Reason #1: We should disciple one another simply because Jesus commands it. Jesus commissioned the church to make disciples in Matthew

28. That answer alone should be sufficient.

Reason #2: We should disciple one another because we care about personal holiness. Christians are new creatures with old habits. We need to help one another break the old habits of our old man and pick up new habits that match our new identity as children of God. Discipling one another is an effective means to that end.

Reason #3: We should disciple one another because we care about our witness to the world. In other words, our discipling is actually connected to the global advance of the gospel!

All authority in heaven and on earth is given to King Jesus so that every nation can hear the good news of the gospel and submit to the King (Matthew 28:18–20). That's what we want—the nations to submit to King Jesus through faith in King Jesus.

What's Jesus' game-plan for this? It's not "Go, therefore, and make converts"; that's a one-time event. It's "Go, therefore, and make disciples"; that's a lifelong process! That's how long it takes to teach these converts how to observe all that the Lord has commanded his people.

The spread of the gospel throughout the world will happen as we obey this call to "make disciples."

THE WHO?

In theory, any professing believer is a candidate for discipling. We cannot disciple unbelievers because they do not have the Holy Spirit (1 Corinthians 2:14). We should evangelize such people.

But notice that I said, "in theory." While any professing believer is a *candidate* for discipling, we are all limited creatures. We can only be in one place at one time, and we cannot be expected to disciple the entire world—or even your entire church.

Speaking of the church, that's where discipling gets *particular*. You and your fellow church members have agreed to the same doctrine, are submitting to the same process of spiritual formation (preaching and shepherding), and have committed to love and walk with the same people.

In our churches, we remind each other that our membership directory is the second most important book after the Bible. The Bible tells us *how* to disciple one another, but the membership directory reminds us *who* we should deliberately disciple. The members of your own local church should be the primary recipients of your discipling effort, as *you* should be the primary recipient of *their* discipling effort.

When every member is seeking to grow in grace together, we live out the reality of what Paul says in Ephesians 4:

> "We are to grow up in every way into him who is the head, into Christ, from whom the whole body, joined and held together by every joint with which it is equipped, when each part is working properly, makes the body grow so that it builds itself up in love." (Eph. 4:15–16).

I don't mean to say you *can't* disciple people who go to another church. I simply want to say that the best and most natural discipling relationships will happen inside the local church.

THE HOW?

Before you say discipling is too hard, I want to leave you with five quick and practical pieces of advice.

1. Pray.

Pray that God would give you a heart that's receptive and bold. Pray that God would lead you to the person or people that you should intentionally grow with in this season.

2. Be intentional (part 1).

Don't suffer from paralysis analysis. Choose a person or two of the same gender and ask them if you could meet on some regular basis to read God's Word, pray together, and hold each other accountable to what you are reading.

3. Be intentional (part 2).

Sometimes, we'll have discipling relationships with people in similar stages of life or with similar life experiences. That's okay. But don't *only* seek out people who are like you. The gospel unites radically different people into one body, and our discipling relationships should reflect the gospel's power to bring radically different people together. Younger men and older men should pair up. Older women and younger women should pair up. Black people and white people and everything in between should pair up. Seek to enter into one another's lives, especially those who are not like you.

4. Learn one another's story.

As you begin a discipling relationship, make sure you know the people around the table. Know their stories. Be a good listener. And be as honest about yourself as wisdom allows. Discipling requires speaking the truth in love, but speaking the truth in love requires that two people know each other enough to be accurate and love each other enough to be genuine.

5. Live life together.

Discipling isn't only about the books we read, or the times we pray. Discipling is also about the battles we fight. So serve the Lord together. If you're single, fold others into your life. If you're married, fold other couples or singles into your life. Spend time together. Hang out. When you do, you'll find many opportunities to experience the ups and downs of life.

Here's the main idea: live life together and keep God's Word at the center. Don't relegate discipling to a one-hour Zoom call. Instead, follow Jesus in real-time as a family. There may be seasons of time where meeting once-a-week for an hour works best. There may be seasons where the only margin you have is to include someone in the routines of your life (I'm thinking of young moms). The goal isn't that we develop an air-tight system. The goal is to love one another as you point each other to God's Word and the power of the gospel. The goal, in a word, is Christ-likeness.

CONCLUSION

You don't need to be a disciple-making guru. You just need to be available. You don't need to be a theologian. You just need to be a means of grace to other disciples.

Disciple-making is for everyday, blood-bought, imperfect followers of Jesus. So, Christian, let's commit to disciple one another!

ABOUT THE AUTHOR

Tony Shepherd is the Associate Pastor of Hampton Roads Fellowship in Newport News, Virginia, and former Christian Hip-Hop producer for Lecrae, Shai Linne, Trip Lee and others. Tony is husband to Jolene, and father to three wonderful sons and a beautiful daughter.

Pray for Other Members

Ty Gooch

Every Christian knows they should pray for others (1 Tim. 2:1). Yet every Christian also knows how terribly trite it feels to ask God over and over again to help out your fellow church members with their health, safety, or money problems. So how do we pray without just repeating ourselves?

Fortunately, God answers this for us. As Christians, we should pray continuously (1 Thess. 5:17), taking each other's anxiety to our caring God (1 Pet. 5:7). We should also pray with thanksgiving, bringing one another's requests to God (Phil. 4:6). The Lord also invites us to pray expectantly for wisdom (James 1:5). We shouldn't grow weary of faithfully praying these prayers. But we can aim for even more precision in our prayers for other church members.

WHAT NOT TO INCLUDE IN PRAYER

But before I get to specifics on what to pray for, let me be specific about how we don't have to pray. Sometimes people make up standards for prayer that simply aren't biblical. The Bible makes it clear that unnecessarily public, lengthy, wordy, and repetitive prayer is not necessarily godly prayer (Matt. 6:6–7). So as we pray for fellow members, don't feel unnecessary guilt that your prayers aren't long. Have clear requests and use few words, trusting that the Lord hears.

WHAT TO INCLUDE IN PRAYER

Instead of heaping up empty phrases in their prayers, Jesus taught his disciples a pattern of prayer that we now call "The Lord's Prayer" (Matt. 6:9–13). We can use this pattern to pray for one another.

1. Adore *God's Name (v. 9)*

Adoring the name of God and asking that God help others adore his name is a great place to start. We should pray that fellow church members would exalt God and delight in his glory.

2. Accept *God's Will (v. 10)*

Much of how we relate to God comes out in responsive humility (Ps. 131). Prayer is one way we express our eager surrender to God's will. We should pray that fellow church members would learn to submit to God's will and trust his providence.

3. Admit *God's Daily Provision (v. 11)*

We need God to provide for our daily sustenance. He works through us and others to see to it that our needs are met through the power of his might and not our own self-reliance. We should pray that God would meet the needs of fellow church members and that they would seek him as the provider of our greatest needs (Matt. 4:4, 6:33).

4. Ask *God's Forgiveness (v. 12)*

We sin daily, whether through commission or omission. How blessed we are to walk in the mercy and grace of God in steadily realigning ourselves with the gospel in prayer. We have a constant opportunity in prayer to confess our sins to the Lord (1 John 1:9). We should pray that God would move others to confess their sins and find hope in the forgiveness of the gospel.

5. Affirm *Forgiveness Toward Others (v. 12)*

We have the privilege of releasing people from relational strife by choosing to forgive them. What a blessing to receive mercy from God in our contriteness and then to offer the same mercy to others (Prov. 28:13, Eph. 4:32). We should pray that fellow members would exercise that same forgiveness toward those that have wronged them.

6. Avoid *Evil* (v. 13)

We're tempted by all kinds of sin (Jas. 1:13–15). There's sin in our own hearts and minds. There's sin imposed on us from the world at the invitation of others (1 John 2:15–17). We need God's protection and a way out of evil, regardless of where it comes from (1 Cor. 10:12–13). We should pray that God would protect fellow members from indwelling sin, the world, and the devil.

Now that we've seen some ways we should pray for others, here are some practical suggestions:

- Pray through a page of your church membership directory during your devotions using the 6 "A's" listed above.
- Before or after Bible study, assign one "A" to each person in the group to pray through for a different church member.
- You can emphasize praying one "A" of the Lord's prayer at mealtime.
- You can pray for one member each night before dinner by focusing on one aspect of the Lord's Prayer for each member. In our home, the awakening aroma of delicious dinner food draws us to the kitchen table out of various tasks each night. On the counter, we have filed away a stack of Christmas cards, which we use to remind us to pray for image-bearing Christian families. I often use an "A" to guide me.

I hope this article gives you a guide to praying more simply and more in line with the Bible's blueprint.

ABOUT THE AUTHOR

Ty Gooch is the senior pastor of Fellowship Life Bible Church in Greater Chicago.

Pursue Wandering Sheep

Jeff Lacine

Christians sometimes fall into temptation and wander from their commitment to Christ. If you've been a Christian for any length of time, you've probably witnessed this sad reality. Maybe you've seen a brother become romantically attached to an unbeliever at his workplace. Rather than answer difficult questions from his Christian friends, he stops gathering with the church altogether. Or maybe you have seen an introverted Christian sister endure trials at home. Instead of seeking out the help she needs from her church out of a desire to follow Christ, she seeks the comfort of isolation. Perhaps you've seen greed and ambition gradually consume a Christian until his love for Christ is marginalized out of existence.

Whether you've seen Christians wander or have wandered yourself, Jesus has some very important words for you to consider in Matthew 18:10–20. In this passage, Jesus teaches us about God's disposition toward wandering Christians and how every Christian, not just the pastors, should pursue wandering sheep and call them to repentance.

SOME CONTEXT

As we seek to unpack Matthew 18:10–20, it is helpful for us to see what's going on in the whole chapter. Matthew 18 contains some of the most well-loved teachings of Jesus: his teaching on becoming like a child (Matthew 18:1–4) and the parable of the lost sheep (18:10–14). Interestingly, these beloved teachings are right next to one of the most challenging and controversial teachings of Jesus—his instructions on church discipline (Matt. 18:15–20).

But the parables aren't randomly organized, as if Jesus just stuck some warm, devotional teachings next to unrelated technical instruction on the fundamentals of church polity. Instead, Matthew 18 presents Jesus teaching us two things: God's disposition toward wandering Christians and the actions Christians should take toward one another.

In Matthew's telling of the parable of the lost sheep, Jesus emphasizes the disposition of the shepherd toward the wandering sheep. We learn that it is not God's will for any of his sheep to wander off and die. ("So it is not the will of my Father who is in heaven that one of these little ones should perish," Matthew 18:14.) He desires that they turn from their wandering and be rescued from danger, welcomed back into the fold with open arms.

How is this love of God for his wandering sheep expressed in real life? Through the church (18:15–20). And it starts with ordinary church members like you and me (18:15).

SOME APPLICATION

So, how do we know when another fellow church member is wandering? How do we pursue them?

First, to know if another church member is wandering, we must know *them*. If you don't feel like you know members of your church well enough to know if they're wandering, then consider these practical ideas.

- Be present when your church gathers on Sunday mornings, and when it gathers at other times (e.g. adult Sunday school, Sunday evening prayer, Wednesday evening Bible study). Come early and linger afterwards. Be intentional about getting to know those who happen to sit around you. Inquire about what first brought them to the church. Ask them about how the sermon impacted them and how they plan to respond. See if they have any prayer requests.

- Pray for members by using your church's membership directory. Perhaps email or call those you are praying for some time during the week to ask them if they have any special prayer requests or needs.
- Serve in the children's ministry. Take interest in the lives of other children's ministry workers and in the lives of the children's parents.
- Join a small group if your church has them. Commit to going regularly and befriending those in the group.
- Familiarize yourself with the other members of your church by working through your church's membership directory and systematically inviting people over for dinner or out for coffee. When you're with them, learn their testimonies and find out how they're presently challenged to grow in Christ.
- Take special initiative in seeking out new members as they join your church, welcoming them into the church family. Take them out for lunch, if you are able, or invite them to your small group or to attend the Bible study or prayer meeting with you.

The more you know people in your church, the more likely it is that you will know if and when they begin to wander. But that's not all! The more you know people in your church, the more likely it is that your question or invitation or e-mail will provoke a conversation that will keep them from wandering in the first place.

RESPONDING TO THE WANDERER

How can you help someone follow Christ when they are wandering into sin?

First and foremost, minister the gospel of grace to them. Remind them of God's love for wandering sheep and offer to support them in their repentance. "I would like to help you with this. How can I best serve you in pursuing Christ right now?" Pray for them and follow up with them. Take them with you to small group or invite them over for dinner, perhaps even encouraging them to share their struggle with others so they can broaden their support in the church. Offer to read a book with them that addresses the issue they are struggling with. Many times, wandering Christians respond very well to this kind of love and support. In such cases, you have gained your brother (18:15) and you should joyfully (18:13) comfort and welcome him with open arms.

But if it becomes clear that a fellow church member is wandering into sin and your individual pursuit of him doesn't work, don't give up. We shouldn't say, "Well, I tried to talk to him and he just won't listen. I wish he would turn from his sin, but it's not up to me, it's between him and God. I need to let it go." No, the Father's heart for his wandering sheep is persistent, his love unfailing. If our attempt to win a wandering Christian fails, we should get more Christians involved (18:16).

At this point, we must be careful to guard against gossip. We shouldn't involve others unless we're certain that the beloved sheep is wandering and has already refused our pursuit. It's important to only share your concern with those who already have a relationship with the church member under consideration. In fact, it's often best to let the wandering Christian know that you're going to share your concern with others.

In most cases, this second step should include an elder. Because if our individual and small group efforts to go after a wandering sheep fail, the elders should lead the church in further pursuit of the wanderer. We should keep going after the wandering sheep until the whole church is involved in the effort (18:17a, "tell it to the church"). *This is the persevering love of God for his wandering sheep on display.*

If the wanderer continues to head into danger (18:17 "if he refuses to listen even to the church"), then the church should lovingly warn him by putting him out of the church (18:17b). Even then, we should still pursue him as we pursue our unbelieving neighbors, family members, and co-workers (i.e., "gentiles and tax collectors").

CONCLUSION

Dear Christian, in Matthew 18:10–20 Jesus isn't merely calling pastors or church leaders to corral wandering sheep. He's calling every church member. In other words, he's calling you.

There are many reasons why Christians sometimes fail to pursue wandering sheep. Perhaps you're not in a position to pursue lost sheep because you're wandering yourself. Perhaps you don't have other Christians going after you because you never committed yourself to a church. Perhaps no one knows you're wandering because you never let anyone know you.

Is it possible that you're reading this article right now because God desires that you wander no longer? Brother, sister, know what it's like to be a known sheep. Commit yourself to a Christian church that will commit themselves to you. Devote yourself to knowing other church members—and *being known* by church members—so that you may display God's love together by pursuing wandering sheep.

ABOUT THE AUTHOR

Jeff Lacine is pastor of Sellwood Baptist Church in Portland, Oregon. He graduated from Bethlehem Seminary. He and his wife have four children.

Forbear with One Another

Dan Miller

Members of the blood-bought church of Jesus Christ have a holy calling to put up with one another. Revel for a moment in that "holy calling" part. In the eternal counsels of God, we were pre-destined to salvation (Eph. 1:3–14). Then, in time, we were grafted into a local body of believers to form a distinct outcropping of Christ's body (1 Cor. 12:12). It's in community that we labor for his eternal kingdom (Col. 3:1–4). Our life together is one of glorious mission.

Now consider that "put up with" bit. It's so earthy you can almost smell the body odor. Bear with one another. Endure your brothers and sisters in Christ as you live together as God's family. Does such a humdrum duty merit more than a passing nod? Bear with me.

Forbearance is more than a nicety we extend to fellow church members when convenient. It's a *moral responsibility*: we are called to clothe ourselves with the virtue of "bearing with one another" in fidelity to Christ (Eph. 4:2; Col. 3:13; cf. Rom. 15:1). It's also a *moral skill*: we must grow wise in putting up with, enduring, patiently abiding, and choosing to live at peace with one another in Christian community.

FORBEARANCE: LOVE IN WORK BOOTS

Forbearance is a viable concept in our culture, but it has a musty smell to it. The prevailing philosophy of Western individualism orients us to develop our personal subset of values. In expressing those values, our world commends aggressive action and efficient accomplishment, even if we must trample others in the process. So your boss may offer a passing word of commendation in a performance review for demonstrating forbearance with others. But you're not likely to leverage such a virtue into a promotion.

The local church, of course, is different. It's a spiritual family in which putting up with one another is a virtue that leads to countless blessings.

As we learn to deploy this virtue, we must face the reality that forbearance is applied primarily in spaces where we encounter believers who bore, annoy, irritate, frustrate, intimidate, exasperate, or just plain make our lives hard. Forbearance certainly happens with easy people. But it flexes its muscles when we relate to people we find difficult.

Invariably, when Christian brothers and sisters bore, annoy, irritate, frustrate, intimidate, or exasperate us, such visceral responses are rooted in our own sinful passions. Forbearance reigns in those passions. It expresses enduring love for people our flesh wants to fight against or flee from. Forbearance is love in work boots. With love, it bears all things and endures all things. With love, forbearance is not arrogant, irritable, or resentful. It unrelentingly puts up with the weaknesses, failures, folly, and off-putting traits, habits, and practices of fellow church members.

This means putting up with that brother whose personality grates against your spirit, and that sister whose preferences never seem to align with yours. It means bearing with that member who talks too much, or processes too slowly. It means enduring that member who loves awkward conversations, that ministry leader who enforces policies you find ridiculous, and that family who touts political views that give you indigestion. It means forbearing with that saint who struggles to break free from an exasperating pattern of sin. It means putting up with that elder who has hurt your feelings or displays weaknesses that frustrate or annoy you. It means choosing to endure biblical sermons, week after week, even when they run longer than you desire or prove less captivating than you wish.

Such church members do not *deserve* your forbearance. They haven't earned it by their exemplary deeds. Indeed, if you plopped them down before some unrestrained unbelievers, they would get an earful. But these same people are your family in Christ, and you are called to put up with them just as they are—at least for now.

FOR NOW, FORBEAR

Indeed, it is this "for now" aspect that upholds forbearance as virtuous. There's admittedly a spiritually anemic, spineless species of tolerance that masquerades as forbearance. Genuine forbearance is virtuous because it zealously imitates the Holy Spirit's sanctifying work in the lives of the redeemed. I put up with him and with her because God is putting up with all of us (Acts 13:18; Rom 2:4). God is slowly chiseling us into the likeness of Christ with all the forbearance of a perfect Father.

Let me put it another way: bearing with other believers is an active partnership with the Holy Spirit. The Father never quits on his children, and the Spirit never ceases to bear with our sins and weaknesses until he has the prize he's after—our conformity to the Son. So when we fail to bear with a church member, we disengage from the Spirit's sanctification efforts and thus grieve him.

FORBEAR, UNTIL WHEN?

Bear with me a little longer.

Our forbearance is incomplete until we recognize that it has a shelf life. The virtue of putting up with sinners can devolve into a vice. God's forbearance is not eternal. The day arrives when his justice renders any further extension of forbearance unjust (Matt 17:17; 25:41–46). So while grace and mercy must fuel persevering love for sinners, local churches must also determine when forbearance has run its course with a member who persists in unrepentant sin.

The tool Christ gives his church for making such a determination is not your personal, unilateral opinion as judge and jury that we've all put up with so-and-so long enough. The tool God provides is corrective church discipline. We must continue to bear with every member of the body until the church determines together that we must all stop doing so. Disciplinary correction constitutes a final extension of forbearance in the hope that the erring member repents and is restored to fellowship (Matt 18:15–20). But it's not until the assembly issues an unheeded call to repentance that we may suspend forbearance.

Until then, we must bear with one another in steadfast love with our eyes set on glory. So when forbearing another church member proves hardest, let us remember the one who chose to love us when we were his enemy (Rom 5:8). Let us remember that he equally chose to love that difficult member. Let us remember that very soon, when we all stand glorified in the presence of our Savior, there will be nothing more to forbear. Love will have won. Forever.

ABOUT THE AUTHOR

Dan Miller is the senior pastor of Eden Baptist Church in Burnsville, Minnesota.

Work for Unity

Harry Fujiwara

Ask any pastor about the things he would most like to see in his church, and somewhere at the top of the list is going to be unity. "Behold, how good and pleasant it is when brothers dwell in unity!" (Psalm 133:1). It *is* good and our churches *do* become more pleasant when they are marked by unity.

And so faithful church members must pursue unity. The Bible calls us to "make every effort to keep the unity of the Spirit through the bond of peace" (Ephesians 4:3, NIV).

But ironically enough, in our pursuit of biblical unity, we can become overly self-focused. We can think of the call to unity as just being about our own individual relationships with other Christians. "Do *I* have any interpersonal conflicts that need to be addressed?" "Am *I* gracious and charitable toward those with differing opinions on secondary and tertiary issues?" "Am *I* joyfully submitting myself to the leadership of the church?" Those are great questions that we should ask ourselves in order that we might, so far as it depends on us, live peaceably with all. But the Scriptural call to unity goes deeper and wider. That is, the Bible sets a higher bar for us than simply not being in conflict with others in our congregation.

And so I want to offer four practical suggestions that will help you work toward unity within your local body. But I'll give you a warning upfront: these aren't easy boxes to check. Some of them require lots of work, others may lead to awkward conversations, and all of them will call you to step out of your comfort zone. But that's why we're commanded to "make every effort" for unity. If it were easy and came naturally, we wouldn't have to be commanded to "make every effort." Nobody has to be told to "make every effort" to eat more potato chips. It's only for eating things like kale that we have to "make every effort."

1. BE A PEACEMAKER.

Being a peacemaker goes beyond just making sure that your own relationships are reconciled. It calls you to encourage and catalyze reconciliation among members who are at odds in your congregation.

When dealing with a potentially unity-disrupting conflict in the church at Philippi, Paul first directly addressed the guilty parties: "I entreat Euodia and I entreat Syntyche to agree in the Lord" (Philippians 4:2). But notice that he doesn't stop there. He then goes on to enlist the help of other members: "Yes, I ask you also, true companion, help these women, who have labored side by side with me in the gospel together with Clement and the rest of my fellow workers, whose names are in the book of life" (Philippians 4:3).

Suppose you know that two members of your church are having a conflict. You could sit back and do nothing—and that would certainly be the easier route to go. But you're called to "make every effort" for unity. What exactly that looks like depends on the situation. In some scenarios, you might call a meeting; in others, you might go to one party and encourage them from the Bible to go and be reconciled. This requires wisdom. But in every case, working for unity means proactively being a peacemaker. And as Jesus said, blessed are the peacemakers.

2. BE A CONNECTOR.

We are, in our sinful nature, cliquish and exclusive. Left to ourselves, we naturally gravitate toward certain people at the expense of broader relationships. But those natural tendencies can be very unhelpful for establishing unity.

So on the most basic level, we need to make sure that we're not simply gravitating toward a single group of friends. Really working for unity calls us to do more—to bring people together as a connector.

Here's an idea on how you can do this: the next time you have a group lunch at your home, invite two people who have completely separate social circles within your church. Allow your home to be the place where they can get to know one another and begin to form a friendship that they may otherwise have never developed.

3. BE A REJOICER AND A WEEPER.

Paul points out that similar to a human body, in the church, "there are many parts, yet one body" (1 Corinthians 12:20). One important inference that he draws from this analogy is that "if one member suffers, all suffer together; if one member is honored, all rejoice together" (1 Corinthians 12:26).

And so very practically, if we are going to work for unity, we need to rejoice with those who rejoice and weep with those who weep (Romans 12:15). Which means attending baby showers and attending funerals. Which means writing notes of congratulations and notes of sympathy. All of that requires us to know each other well enough that we are actually aware when our brother or sister is rejoicing or weeping, which again involves intentional effort. Being with your church members in the highs and lows of their lives will go a long way toward building a greater, more enduring unity.

4. BE GOSPEL-CENTERED.

Most importantly, if you're going to work for unity in your church, you need to be gospel-centered.

Through the gospel, each member of your church has been united to Christ. Therefore, each member of your church is united to one another. Note how Paul specifically points out that the believers at Philippi—the ones who really needed to make every effort for unity in their body—all have their names in the book of life (Philippians 4:3). Given that we're all going to spend eternity together worshipping our common Savior as fellow citizens of heaven, unity in the here and now is something worth fighting for!

We must remember the gospel. Because it's only by the power of the gospel that such an eclectic church like yours (and like mine!) can be brought together by a common interest and demonstrate true love and unity. In fact, it's this love and unity that then empowers the church's gospel ministry "with one mind striving side by side for the faith of the gospel" (Philippians 1:27).

So, brothers and sisters, go and make every effort to pursue unity. I know it's hard. But it's good for you. Like eating more kale.

ABOUT THE AUTHOR

Harry Fujiwara is the senior pastor of First Baptist Manhattan in New York City.

"Speak Only What is Good to Give Grace"

Josh Manley

Take a glance at Twitter, cable news, or your most active group texts. To say that kind words have been in short supply over the past year would be an understatement. On any number of issues, consider how many words people have deployed to divide rather than reconcile, to hurt rather than heal, to demean rather than lift up. Sticks and stones still break bones, but you can't tell me words don't hurt.

From your computer to your church to your kitchen table, what's been your strategy for choosing your words this year? As those who confess and serve the God who speaks, who created the world by his Word, and whose Word gives life, have we forgotten how eternally important and powerful the gift of speech is? After all, the Triune God has revealed himself through his words. In Christ, he has freed us to use our speech for astonishing and enduring ends.

HOW DO I KNOW THIS? THE BOOK OF EPHESIANS.

Ephesians begins with soaring expressions of God's sovereignty over all things (1:11). Paul shows us God's election of and love for his people from before the foundation of the world (1:4). He considers how God raises us from spiritual death to spiritual life (2:1–5). He unfolds how God includes us in his cosmic plans to unite not just Jew and Gentile

(2:15) but all things in Christ (1:10). In Ephesians, Paul leads us to the breathtaking mountaintop vistas of God's glory.

And yet, he doesn't leave us there. He calls us to respond—or, more specifically, to speak. Paul draws out for us how God's great work of redemption in Christ transforms our lives, and in so doing transforms our speech. Paul writes in Ephesians 4:29: "Let no corrupting talk come out of your mouths, but only such as is good for building up, as fits the occasion, that it may give grace to those who hear."

Read that again! Ephesians teaches that God's glorious purposes for the universe and his people in Christ extend to our speech. Apart from faith in Christ, sinful hearts spew words that amplify the death and decay of the fallen world. But now in Christ we can use our speech to give what was previously impossible: grace.

Let's consider *two* ways this teaching should shape our speech.

1. GOD USES YOUR SPEECH FOR ENDS YOU CAN'T FULLY FATHOM.

I bet you can easily recount words that have hurt you. But I hope you can also remember times when a fellow Christian spoke intentionally to build you up—when someone surprised you with a kind response when you expected a harsh word or shared the gospel with you when you felt far from God. In those ordinary moments, God did something eternally glorious through your brother or sister's speech. He used those believers to speak what is good in order to give grace.

What if we really believed our words could give grace? I suspect we would start to look for ways to deploy our words for this eternally good end. What if—based on Ephesians 4:29—we looked at our church's weekly gathering as an indispensable opportunity to speak good into the lives of others? Given what we read here in Ephesians, the God who speaks must get particular glory by using the words of his redeemed people to accomplish goals that we cannot fully fathom on this side of eternity.

We don't yet comprehend the extent of God's grace to his children, but we know he uses our speech to extend a measure of grace.

2. GOD USES YOUR SPEECH FOR WHAT LASTS.

If we took an inventory of everything we wasted over the last year, how many words would make the list?

As with any other scarce resource, even the most verbose have a limited amount of words in a lifetime. What a tragedy it would be to come to the end of our lives and realize that we wasted our words on speech that had no lasting value.

But if we speak what is good to give grace, then God uses our ordinary words for his extraordinary purposes. He even uses them to build his people together into his dwelling place in the age to come (2:22). In Christ, God means to use our speech to build what lasts.

We shouldn't reduce this command to mere positivity or flattery. The speech that gives grace is saturated in the gospel! This means sometimes delivering a hard word when it's appropriate because that will do the most eternal good. It means apologizing when we're wrong or encouraging someone in their gifts, even when that means ours take a backseat.

Consider what a wonderfully countercultural place our local churches would be if we all strategically planned to use words for what will be celebrated on the last day. God's Christ-exalting, universe-transforming, destiny-shifting plans in Christ include deploying our words for eternal ends. In this present cultural moment where words seem to be many but good ones seem so few, let's make it our ambition to spend the years the Lord gives us speaking what is good to give grace.

My generation was rightly summoned, "Don't waste your life!" In order to fulfill that call, we need to hear another one "Don't waste your words!"

Our days and our words are numbered, and before long we will have to give an account to God for how we used them. His words are always true, always good, and never wasted. As his children, may the words we speak bring glory to his great name and grace to all his people.

ABOUT THE AUTHOR

Josh Manley is a Pastor of RAK Evangelical Church in the United Arab Emirates.

Put Others Interests Above Your Own

Brian Vickers

C oming up with a list of what makes a good church member seems like an easy enough thing to do—until you try it. At the top of that list, of course, is "believe in Jesus for the forgiveness of sins." What comes next? What sort of actions, characteristics, and attitudes would you list second and third and fourth?

The potential danger with such a list is that the things further down the line will perhaps seem *less* necessary, provided we think we have what's *most* important. But the real danger is that a list of what makes a good church member may easily turn into a performance checklist—something by which we weigh our successes or failures in the balance of boxes ticked. With that said, there is a text that I put at the top of the list and that likely sums up most of whatever else we might include. That text is Philippians 2:1-4:

If, then, there is any encouragement in Christ, if any consolation of love, if any fellowship with the Spirit, if any affection and mercy, make my joy complete by thinking the same way, having the same love, united in spirit, intent on one purpose. Do nothing out of selfish ambition or conceit, but in humility consider others as more important than yourselves. Everyone should look not to his own interests, but rather to the interests of others. (CSB)

Here Paul shows what life looks like for citizens of heaven (Phil 1:27); those who live in the hope that God will complete his work of salvation (Phil 1:6); those who have righteousness—that is, Jesus himself—purely as a gift from God (Phil 3:9). Ultimately, the life Paul desires for the Philippians, and for us, is a life that reflects Christ who, rather than using his person and power for himself, became a servant who gave his life for us (Phil 2:6–8). For church members, love and service flowing from unity in Christ are not added virtues or the trickle-down effects of sound doctrine.

Living for others is living as Christ—hardly just another item on a list.

IF YOU ARE CHURCH MEMBERS...

Paul's exhortation to put aside self-centered ambition and personal gain in exchange for putting others first flows from the unity believers have (or at least should have) in Christ. When Paul says, "If there is any encouragement . . . consolation . . . fellowship . . . compassion and mercy," he's saying, "Since there is . . ." It's kind of like a parent saying, "If you've ever heard me say anything, then hear this."

The exhortations in verses 2–4 aren't more things to do or add to a baseline of what it means to be a believer (or a church member) but show how the reality of verse 1 is expressed. In other words, the exhortations aren't just good if and when we get around to them. They're not icing on the cake of salvation but part and parcel of the reality of salvation. Notice also that Paul's joy will be fulfilled through seeing the Philippians living for each other (2:2). All in all, the church at Philippi was a relatively healthy church. But Paul is concerned about more than beginnings—his pastoral joy comes in seeing the Philippians grow in God's on-going work of salvation as they display Christ for one another.

...THEN YOU WILL SHOW CHRIST TO ONE ANOTHER

When you look at Philippians chapter 2, your eyes likely will drift to verses 5–11 (thanks in part to Bible headings). This is understandable to a degree since these verses contain some of

Paul's highest and most concentrated Christology. Paul, however, might be surprised to find that we often unpack verses 5-11 in minute detail but sometimes pay little attention to the verses right before.

We must guard against abstracting the Christology of verses 5–11 from the context. At the same time, we must avoid over-reacting, as some do these days, and only emphasize Christ's example in verses 5–11. Happily, we don't have to choose either/or. When we choose both/and we'll have a greater appreciation for all eleven verses. If we want to know what it looks like to prefer others more than ourselves and to seek the good of others over our own good, then we need look no further than verses 5–11. Good church members will look at others the way Christ regarded them—as people in need of love and service.

PUTTING OTHERS FIRST: MINISTERING CHRIST TO EACH OTHER

When it comes to living out Paul's teaching in Philippians 2, we cannot simply respond with, "Yes, I need to be less selfish," or "I need to be less self-absorbed," or "I need to put others first," and then resolve to make some changes. Of course, we must consciously and deliberately put others first. But if we take this expression of the gospel of Christ and turn it into *what we must do*, then the Christian life becomes a matter of performance. Worse, it potentially makes us view others as objects for fulfilling a personal checklist of what it means to be a good church member. If I live for others as an attempt to show that I'm walking in obedience, then I'm still living for myself.

So where do we begin? First, we need to let the text do its work of exposing how we fail to live for others—how we are selfish and self-centered. We begin with confession without excuses and justifications. If we're honest, these verses will bring a certain amount of fear and trembling. At the same time, we turn (or better, *we are turned*) to the hope of the gospel, the finished work of Christ the Lord and King (2:9-11) in whom we are righteous (3:9). In this way, we receive 2:1–4 as a gift that sets us free from the self-absorbed ambition that holds us back from fellowship and service to one another in Christ.

We're all familiar with Philippians 2:12: "Work out your salvation with fear and trembling." We need to put that together with 2:1–4." Living united in fellowship of the Spirit, living for, and serving one another as Christ served, is what it looks like to work out our salvation—the salvation that God began in us and promises to complete (1:6). The work of love and service cannot be "done" apart from believing that it is God who works in us according to his will and purpose (2:13). It is his salvation work in us. As we're called to look away from ourselves to God in Christ alone for salvation, so we are turned away from ourselves to serve one another as good church members.

ABOUT THE AUTHOR

Brian is Professor of New Testament Interpretation at The Southern Baptist Theological Seminary and a member of Sojourn Church, Jeffersontown Kentucky.

Rejoice with Those Who Rejoice; Weep with Those Who Weep

Paul Martin

Dear Ones,

2 Thessalonians 1:3 We ought always to give thanks to God for you, brothers, as is right, because your faith is growing abundantly, and the love of every one of you for one another is increasing.

What a joy it has been for me to watch your love for one another abound and grow in this season of trial. Like the furnace that burns the dross and leaves the precious metal, your godliness is showing, and it is beautiful. Now, I want to call on you to excel even more in your pure love for one another.

Romans 12:15 Rejoice with those who rejoice, weep with those who weep.

You are doing a great job at weeping with those who weep. You know what it means to enter into the sorrows of your fellow members and help carry their burdens, even in that uniquely quiet, Canadian way. You're not showy about it.

In fact, most of it I only hear about much later and usually second-hand—the best kind of gossip.

When members have suffered, you have cried with them, sent them text messages full of hope and empathy, written cards, delivered meals (a LOT of meals!), and done what might be best—prayed. I love being the member of a praying church. Prayer itself is a kind of declaration of faith. When we pray, we are actually spending our time seeking God on behalf of another, instead of just doing all those practical things. Oh, the practical things are great and important, but they are not *most* important. You seem to have that figured out.

I wonder if some of our strength at weeping with those who weep comes from living in the West? We are not lacking much, and our lives are comparatively easy. Perhaps our ability to weep with those who weep stems in part from our ability to tap into lots of resources with which to help? Or maybe it's just our all-too-familiar experiences with suffering? None of us gets through life without troubles and trials. Either way, this church does a good job of weeping with those who weep.

Romans 12:15 Rejoice with those who rejoice…

Now, this second bit of authentic love seems to me to be a bit more complex. To rejoice in someone else's joy sounds great—until yet another girlfriend announces her engagement and you haven't gone on a single date in three years. I mean, you are happy for her, you really are. But it's not easy to enter into her joy.

Imagine being at a professional hockey game for one of those free giveaways, a really good giveaway like a new car, something you really want. And they call the Blue Seats (your color!), Section 321 (your section!), Row B (your row!), and, finally, Seat 32. But you are Seat 33. Does your heart soar with delight for the total stranger who's been stealing your armrest all game? Are you overflowing with joy that he—not you—won the new car?

Rejoice with those who rejoice! He's rejoicing. Are you?

I mean, if it had been a dude in the Red Seats, Section 481, well, that distance probably would have eased the disappointment. And that's precisely my point. The closer people are to us makes our rejoicing with them more difficult.

We're all experts at jealousy and envy. Isn't it interesting how we don't have to practice those in order to be good at them? We know how to want what others get and how to angrily hope they lose what they got, even if we never get it! Our deceitful hearts can even launch into full on "discovery mode," searching out everything we can come up with that's wrong with the "winner" in order to justify our hate and anger and disappointment.

Rejoice with those who rejoice.

This really is the heart of love, isn't it? When she gets engaged, when he wins the car, the loving heart looks with a bountiful eye and discovers deep happiness in the good of another. Love requires total self-forgetfulness and other-centeredness.

Romans 12:9 Let love be genuine. Abhor what is evil; hold fast to what is good.

Paul begins his grocery list of attributes of genuine love in Romans 12 with an odd pairing. He says that authentic love *starts* with a heart that actively despises evil and clings to what is good. In other words, before we can show our love outwardly, we have to pay attention to the focused affections of our heart. To put it starkly, if you are looking at pornography, you will have a harder time loving the saints. Pornography is evil. It must be utterly rejected and despised. You must wash the lust and sexual immorality out of your life like a surgeon scrubs her hands before surgery.

This makes sense because God is love. And all his acts toward his own flow out of this endless love. He loved the world so much that he sent his only Son to die for his people. Our self-existent, self-giving God gave all. One might say that to love is to want what is best for the other. More than that, it is to be willing *to do whatever it takes* to ensure that best for the other.

If we are clinging to what is good—God, his Word, etc.—and rejecting outright what is evil—the world, our flesh, and the devil—then we will be in the right posture to look at the dude sitting too close and say, "Congratulations, man! You won the car!" And to say that with authentic joy in our hearts. You will be able to look at that newly engaged sister and say something similar. And mean it. Even though you might be a tad sad as you do.

> Proverbs 14:10
> The heart knows its own bitterness,
> and no stranger shares its joy.

Did not our Lord himself know sorrow in the joy of laying down his life for us? On this side of the Jordan, all love seems to carry with it the scent of sorrow.

To really love another is a spiritual exercise. It requires massive internal commitment to kill every visible sin, to resist every temptation, to cling to every good, and to reject every evil. This love flows out of death: death to sin, to self, to the ways of Satan, and to our own sullied desires. But it's beautiful to behold.

When you truly rejoice with the sister who is rejoicing, you're declaring to the world there is a God and he is your ultimate satisfaction. Brothers and sisters, abound in this love! Grow in it. Seek it. Practice it. Risk failing at it in order to do it. Pray to God, trust his grace, and open wide your heart to your fellow brothers and sisters.

As you do, "the God of love and peace will be with you" (2 Corinthians 13:11 ESV). And you will learn by experience that it really is better to give than to receive.

> 2 Corinthians 13:14
> The grace of the Lord Jesus Christ and the love of God and the fellowship of the Holy Spirit be with you all. (ESV)

Amen.

With much love for you,
Pastor Paul

ABOUT THE AUTHOR

Paul Martin is a pastor of Grace Fellowship Church in Toronto, Ontario.

Associate with the Lowly

Joel Kurz

Francis Grimké thundered against a church that had lost her way. The year was 1898, and the pastor called his church to repent of its hypocrisy. He said:

> The pulpit should be a tower of strength to every weak cause. Women should hasten to church, saying—Our cause will be upheld there. Homeless little children should speed to the sanctuary, saying—We will be welcomed there. Slaves running away should open the church door with certainty of hospitality.[3]

Grimké's point is simple: society's lowly should find solace in the church.

Is this true in your own life? Is this true in your church? Do you associate with the lowly?

WHO ARE THE LOWLY?

"Lowly," for the purpose of this article, refers to societal outcasts. The lowly are those upon whom society frowns. *In-groups* and *out-groups* are nothing new. By the time a child arrives in middle school, she

3   Grimke, Frances J. (Francis James) *The Negro His Rights and Wrongs, The Forces for Him and Against Him,* Cornell University Library, 1898

discovers an entire caste system. From the schools to the streets, from the backrooms to the board rooms, from the neighborhoods to the nations: you are either *in* or *out*.

Outcasts change according to our time and place. In Jesus' day, there were a number of outcasts with whom he boldly associated:

> *Ethnic Outcasts:* Jesus speaks of a *good* Samaritan and shows kindness to the Samaritan woman at the well.

> *Moral Outcasts:* Jesus halts the stoning of a woman caught in adultery and shows forgiveness.

> *Ceremonial Outcasts:* Lepers come to Jesus, and a dangerous demoniac runs to him.

> *Imperial Outcasts:* A Roman centurion places faith in Jesus as Jesus declares that he has more faith than all of Israel. Jesus invites a tax collector into his inner circle. [4]

4 It's easy to romanticize the "outcasts" of Jesus' day. We wonder, "How could these Pharisees have been so hard on them?" We must tread with humility. Rome dominated

JESUS AND HUMILITY

Jesus describes himself as lowly (Matt. 11:29). We must remember that humility was not a virtue in Jesus' day.[5] The same term is often used to reference a status of low degree (Romans 12:16, James 1:9). In Jesus' humility, he associated with the outcast. He took on a *lower status*. Christians are called to do the same.

So, why wouldn't we associate with the lowly? Mainly because of our pride. Pharisaic religion is filled with pride and, as a result, filled with disdain toward the outcast.

Proud people will not associate with the lowly, for a few reasons:

1. Pride seeks honor.

Pride says, "I deserve God's love, others don't." In today's social media culture, we're filled with self-absorbed braggadocios who demand

Israel requiring huge taxes. Tax collectors were Jews who sold out their own people for selfish gain. I may have easily sided with the Pharisees who were fighting for the dignity and rights of their people.

5   Thinkers and writers such as John Dickson, in *Humilitas*, have sought to show that the modern concept of humility actually comes from the person, work, and life of Jesus. In the Roman empire, the opposite was true. Virtue was to seek one's own honor and status.

entitlement. In Luke 14, Jesus is invited to the home of a Pharisee. He notices the jockeying for position that's going on and so he says, "When you are invited, go and sit in the lowest place" (14:10).

Humility doesn't seek its own honor. Christians don't live for social praise. What your neighbor thinks of your car, your house, your furniture, and your friends should not matter to you. What matters is *not* our display of hope in a world that fades, but rather our display of hope in a world to come.

2. Pride seeks self-benefit.

As Luke 14 continues, Jesus turns to the man who invited him and rebukes his guest list:

> When you give a dinner or a banquet, do not invite your friends or your brothers or your relatives or rich neighbors, lest they also invite you in return and you be repaid. But when you give a feast, invite the poor, the crippled, the lame, the blind, and you will be blessed, because they cannot repay you. For you will be repaid at the resurrection of the just. (14:12–14)

The proud invite friends who will prove to be a benefit. They invite those who are known to bring a good dessert. They invite good conversation partners. They invite those who will make them look good. They invite for *self-benefit*. In contrast, love does not seek its own.

In a horrific turn of events, Jesus eventually tells us the proud are shut out from the eternal dinner (Luke 14:24).

WHO'S COMING OVER TO DINNER?

Jesus went to the outcasts, and we are called to do the same. James 2:1–7 resolutely condemns showing partiality toward the rich—in other words, the *in-group*. The rich need Jesus as much as the poor. Jesus doesn't call you to associate with the lowly and to avoid the rich. Instead, he calls us all to impartiality.

Here's a case study: It's Sunday morning. There are two guests at your church service. The first is a young professional. He's new to your town, works at some kind of firm, and his wife is beginning her residency. They're looking for a new church home. The other visitor is a single mom from the housing projects down the street. She's clearly disheveled and poor. Feeling a bit out of place, she takes a seat in the corner and quietly sits alone.

Question: In your church, who is most likely to receive a lunch invitation? Which visitor will spark excitement? Who is swarmed after the service? Who's coming over to dinner that week?

While many of us *think* of our churches as welcoming places, I wonder if we subconsciously violate James 2:1–7. I wonder if they are welcome to some and decidedly *not welcome* to others.

It's worth asking the question: in our hospitality and our affection, do we show partiality? We remember the names of the upper-middle class couple. We even know where they attended undergrad. Yet we never found the time to get the name of that single mom from the projects. And this has happened more than once.

LET US NOT SHOW FAVORITISM

The application is simple: make it your goal to associate with the lowly. Who are the outcasts in your community? Who is overlooked? And when are they coming over for dinner?

Praise God that he didn't avoid us. Who are the lowly? Those who have no other option but Jesus. Jesus said, "Blessed are the poor in spirit, for theirs is the kingdom of heaven" (Matt. 5:3). The Apostle Paul, though he wrote much of the New Testament and was God's chief apostle to the Gentiles, considered himself the worst of sinners. All who come to Christ view themselves in this way. We are spiritual scoundrels who were found by a sufficient and merciful Savior. We've been saved by God's love, so we who were at one time spiritual outcasts must go to societal outcasts and show that same love.

CONCLUSION

I'll close with a few words of thankfulness for members from my own church. Eric and Aisha moved into a depressed neighborhood to display gospel-motivated hospitality among the forgotten. Mike and Bekah systematically invite drug dealers into their homes for dinner. Bethany visited an elderly woman in an assisted living complex and loved her through her final days. Alton and Mike made an effort to know and love all the neighbors on their tough little block in Baltimore. Carde chooses to associate with the homeless after church instead of small talk with friends.

This is not "us serving them." This is not the "Haves" helping the "Have-Nots". Rather we say: "There is no "us and them." There's only a bunch of lowly people, seeking to do good to *everyone* for the sake of Christ.

ABOUT THE AUTHOR

Joel Kurz is the lead pastor of The Garden Church in Baltimore, Maryland.

Imagination Required: Enter into the Trials of Fellow Church Members

Derek Minton

What if I told you a healthy imagination was essential to being a good church member? You may think I need to read less Lewis and Tolkien and more 9Marks. But I'm serious. Imagination not only provides a door into the fanciful world of fairy tales; it also provides a pathway to understanding the pain and perplexities of fellow church members.

Cultural clichés hint at this point: "She lives vicariously through her children," we say. We've even coined words to describe this imaginative ability. An "escapist" is a person who seeks distraction and relief from unpleasant realities by imagining themselves living a different life, often someone else's.

As believers, our imaginations have been redeemed. They're no longer primarily a way of escaping into the unreal, but rather a way of entering into the realities of fellow suffering saints.

SCRIPTURE REQUIRES IT

The Bible is full of commands to do this:

- *Weep* with those who weep (Rom. 12:15).
- Remember those in prison *as though in prison with them* (Heb. 13:3).
- *Bear* one another's burdens (Gal. 6:2).
- Consider how to stir one another up and encourage one another (Heb.10:24–25).

These commands implicitly require that we to some extent feel the grief of the stillborn, the paralysis of prison, the burden of our brother's struggle with sin. When Hebrews exhorts us to consider, it's exhorting us to imagine. The writer is commanding us to envisage our brother's or sister's situation such that we, with the help of the Spirit, are able to stir them up to love and good works. In order to do this fully and fruitfully, we must remember: If one member suffers, all suffer together (1 Cor. 12:26).

As we encounter suffering saints in our church, we often think: *I need wisdom for this conversation.* We don't want to ask the wrong question or say the wrong thing. I'd like to suggest that good questions come less often from spontaneous wisdom and more often from taking the time to think or imagine our way into someone else' trials.

COME IMAGINE WITH ME

Let's do some imagining together. Does someone in your church deal with chronic pain? Let's imagine what their life is like.

Have you ever gotten your fingers shut in your front door? What if you couldn't get them out? There you sat in the foyer on the floor. Everyone has made suggestions, and you've tried them all, but still your fingers are stuck. For months, you keep a hopeful attitude. "Maybe tomorrow will be better?" you say to yourself.

Three months go by and you start to get used to your predicament. The pain, however, is only part of it. You miss doing things you used to do: working, going on dates with your wife, taking your children to the park, teaching Sunday School. You tell yourself, "It's okay. Things are just different now. I just have to find a new normal." So you do. You find a new way to date your wife, play with your children, and serve the church.

But going to work is out of the question. You can't "go to work" with your fingers in the door. So you start dreaming about how you could work from home if you could learn to type quickly with one hand. Or maybe you could buy some voice recognition software. After several months of failed attempts, you give up on that idealistic mirage.

Your new normal means a new normal for your family. Your children and wife are doing their best to acclimate. Their expectations are slowly recalibrating. You enjoy playing with your children for 15 minutes; you even forget about your fingers for a while. But before too long, after all that moving around and having fun, the pain increases.

Your wife is doing her best. She has a good attitude about taking care of all the family responsibilities. Plus, she's taking care of you now, too. You can no longer get dressed, take a shower, or even cut your toenails. She gets dressed up for your "door dates" even though you can't go anywhere. Most difficult for her, though, is your inability to listen to her. Coping with the pain commandeers your concentration.

Your doctor tries to help. She prescribes medication and various remedies. But none of it can actually get your fingers out of the door.

As the months pass, you start to notice that the medication has some negative effects. It distorts your personality. It makes you feel hungover in the mornings. It ruins your ability to concentrate; it stokes nightmares. But without it, you can't be a dad or a husband in any meaningful since because the days of being used to the pain are long gone.

By now, you're worn-down. You just want your fingers out of the door. And if one more well-meaning church member—who has both their hands in their pockets and a smile on their face—says, "How's your pain today?" you might just lose it!

A FEW PRINCIPLES

A few principles that apply to both short-term and long-term suffering.

First, "the problem" is not the primary problem.

Take the guy who loses his job and remains unemployed for a while. The ensuing trial is not the loss of his job *per se*. More meaningful is the fact that he no longer has the money to pay his mortgage. His family no longer enjoys financial stability. Inwardly, he now lacks purpose—particularly if his unemployment is prolonged. He feels defeated by the deafening silence of waiting for yet another response to his resume.

Second, take the burden of the question on yourself.

When we ask a suffering saint, "How are you doing?" or "How was your week?" we are inadvertently asking *them* to do the "considering." These questions may indicate that we haven't genuinely considered their predicament. We see them in the church hallway. We know they're not doing well, so we say the first thing that comes to mind. We know from experience that inexact questions like "how was your week?" are notoriously difficult to answer. Who walks around with their whole week inside their head? Plus, it can hardly

be answered genuinely while scurrying through the foyer on your way to Sunday School.

Third, don't turn the person into the problem.

Our go-to question for someone in a trial is often: How was your "so-and-so" this week? While they've probably been asked about their cancer or their Crohn's multiple times that week, no one has likely asked them how they're doing spiritually. But remember: your brother is not his burden. Your sister is not her suffering. They're Christians who are experiencing a trial, and they are fighting for their spiritual health.

So ask them if they've been able to read their Bible this week. That question provides an opportunity to get their mind off their problem and to encourage you with what he's been thinking about from Scripture. Or perhaps he'll tell you how his Crohn's makes it difficult for him to concentrate or read. That will help you to pray for him, and to ask more specific questions in the future.

Fourth, leave room for lament.

Just as a poor atmosphere makes it hard to breathe, a poor question can make it hard for a sister to truthfully tell you how she's doing. When we haven't imagined ourselves into our struggling sister's situation, when we haven't felt her frustration, our questions can give off an air of positivity that communicates our lack of consideration.

Conversely, faithful consideration helps us do away with the unspoken expectation that our sister should have something positive to report. It opens the door to hopeful lament. When positivity pervades, those in the midst of trial will rightly or wrongly feel like you don't "get it." When we, however, allow ourselves to be burdened through imagination, our questions will come with a solemnity that often not only opens the door to lament but also to praise.

Fifth, remember people aren't silos.

Our suffering normally causes suffering for those we love. Remember the brother who lost his job? Encourage your wife to write his wife a card with Matthew 6:25ff

in it. Create space for your wife to take her to coffee and to find out how she's doing and if they need help financially.

Last, always consider but rarely compare (at least out loud).

When considering someone else's suffering, we often compare it with our past experiences out of a good desire to identify with them. This practice rarely encourages people in the midst of suffering. Remember the fingers-in-the-door illustration? After about the 6-month mark, how helped do you think you'd be by someone saying, "You know what, I got my fingers stuck in the door one time"?

CAVEAT AND CONCLUSION

Am I saying that you need to imagine and feel the detailed trials of each and every one of your fellow church members as you pray though your church membership directory? No. We are finite; we can only do so much. God knows we are dust.

But I *am* suggesting that faithfulness requires that we don't content ourselves with holding the body's pains, burdens, and sorrows at arm's length. Faithful consideration requires imaginative contemplation (Heb. 10:25). If Paul's words, "If one member suffers, all suffer together" are realized in our churches, it will be through the labor of Spirit-empowered imagination.

ABOUT THE AUTHOR

Derek Minton is a member of Heritage Baptist Church in Owensboro, KY

Invite Your Pastors into Your Life

Omar Johnson

What's your relationship like with your pastors? Non-existent? Distant? Cordial? Warm? Now, a follow-up question: who do you think is responsible for improving or investing in that relationship?

I know how a lot of church members would respond to that question: "Of course it's *their* job!"

Some church members expect their pastors to do all the pursuing and all the follow-up. They're instinctively supposed to know what's going on with everyone at all times. But one-way relationships are draining; they're frustrating. We should aim for something better.

The point of this article is simple: church members should pursue their pastors. And by "pastors," plural, I mean to suggest that church members not simply pursue meaningful spiritual contact with their senior pastor or lead pastor, but with the pastors or elders in general (the NT uses the terms interchangeably) in their churches. To that end, what follows works best in a church where a plurality of elders exists, where multiple men share the load in shepherding the flock. My suggestion is that you prayerfully open up your life to at least one of them, for both your and their spiritual good.

I'll offer two reasons why members should invite their pastors into their life, and then close with a rapid-fire list of suggestions for how to do it effectively.

TWO REASONS

1. You need your pastors.

Christians often suffer from two common misconceptions.

Some Christians think, "All I need is Jesus." At face value, this sentiment seems to exalt the sufficiency of Christ to care for and strengthen his people. But Christians sometimes use this phrase to reject any pastoral prying. Maybe they shoo their pastors away to keep hiding a secret sin. Maybe the messiness of their problems embarrasses them, so they stiff-arm their shepherds and share their hardships with Jesus and Jesus alone.

When Christians do this, they neglect one of the primary means that Christ established to care for and strengthen them—their church and their elders. Remember, Jesus designed the church to be a people who testify of him and who help each other properly reflect him (Matt. 16:16–18; 18:15–18).

But that's not all. Jesus also gave the church pastors to edify, equip, and encourage the church (Eph. 4:11–12). Pastors are God's gifts to God's people to help them grow in godliness. Why would you want to keep such a gift at arm's length?

On the other hand, some Christians think just *any* pastor will do. In our age of podcasted and live-streamed preachers, it's easy—almost effortless, really—to seek guidance from every pastor but your own. In that way, you might acknowledge the fact that you need *a* pastor. But if that's you, know this: you don't just need *a* pastor, you need *your* pastor.

How do I know? Because the sovereign God who determines our times and places (Acts 17:26) put you in your church led by those men. God knew that you'd be wrestling with this or that theological issue, marital struggle, sexual temptation, or relational conflict, and he made sure to have you in this church led by these pastors that he's raised up to help you.

So brothers and sisters, tap into this rich resource. Reach out to your pastors and invite them into your life. You need them.

2. Your pastors need you.

A pastor should be tied to the people the Lord has given him to lead. That's why Peter says, "Shepherd the flock of God that is *among you*" (1 Pet 5:2). Pastors are to be *among* their people, involved in their lives, engaged in their experiences.

What does that mean for you? It means that you help your pastors faithfully do their job by inviting them into your life—to weep with you in pain, to rejoice with you through progress, to pray with you in distress, to plead with you when drifting.

These moments remind pastors that God expects them to shepherd sheep throughout the week, not simply pump out sermons on Sundays. But they do more than that. They also encourage your pastors to keep going in ministry, as they see first-hand that their labor is not in vain.

Finally, recent scandals involving various ministry leaders highlight the danger of living a secret life. I can't help but wonder how things might have happened differently if these men had spent real time getting to know their people. Who knows? Perhaps your transparency before your pastors would model for *them* how *they* ought to live. Perhaps it might even convict them of their lack of transparency and help them live with integrity before you and others.

So brothers and sisters, don't let your pastors live on a ministry island. Let them get to know you, and the Lord's love for them through you. They need you.

21 RAPID-FIRE IDEAS

Let me close by offering 21 brief ideas to build a relationship with your pastors. These certainly aren't exhaustive, and aren't meant to be prescriptive, but they will get you started. The point is not to use this list as a sure-fire way to get more of your pastors' attention or time. Elders are busy pastoring the entire congregation, let alone caring for their own families and souls. In other words, temper your expectations. Don't demand more of them, rather swing open the door of your life that they might know more of you. So as you invite a pastor or multiple pastors into your life, here are some suggestions:

1. Share prayer requests with him weekly.
2. Text or email him questions during the week that you may have on the text he will be preaching.
3. Ask follow-up questions from the sermon, or note specific things from the sermon you were encouraged or challenged by.
4. Invite him and his wife to breakfast. Or lunch. Or dinner. Or coffee.
5. Make him one of your first calls when tragedy hits.
6. Share with him that you prayed for him that morning.
7. Share something encouraging from your quiet time.
8. Confess sins to him.
9. Call him in the midst of temptation.
10. Ask him if he wants to go for a run or play ball.
11. Ask if you can hang out and read in his office while he works.
12. Invite your friends to church and introduce them to him.
13. Ask his counsel on major decisions—if you're thinking about moving, switching jobs, visiting another church, pursuing a spouse, etc.
14. Tell him about the movies and shows you watch, and the songs you listen to.
15. Tell him what you're reading.
16. Share one of your hobbies with him and ask if he'd be interested in trying it.
17. Tell him when your birthday is.
18. Tell him something of your family background.
19. Be super elaborate in your membership interview about your testimony and upbringing. Let him know a lot about you upfront.
20. Share how you're processing events in the news or in the community.
21. Send him funny gifs and memes!

Brothers and sisters, it really is that simple: invite your pastors into your life.

ABOUT THE AUTHOR

Omar Johnson is the senior pastor of Temple Hills Baptist Church in Temple Hills, Maryland.

Encouraging Your Pastor

Chad Van Dixhoorn

There are books that tell you how to take care of your children, your spouse, your house, or your dog. There appears to be no end of books that tell you how to look after yourself. There are books to aid teachers in helping students, lawyers in defending clients, or pastors in caring for church members.

But where do we find the books that tell us how to look after those who look after us? How to help your mother train you in godliness. Six steps to your doctor's happiness. Looking after your teacher. Loving your lawyer. I'm not confident we would benefit from all these titles, but one book I can't find that I'm certain *would* be useful is something on how to encourage your pastor.

PAY FOR YOUR PASTORS

Perhaps the book can't be found because it's never been written. But it would be a book worth writing—and for all of us, worth reading. After all, Scripture reminds us to honor elders that rule well, but especially to honor "those who labor in preaching and teaching" (1 Tim. 5:17). Such honor can take many forms: respect, encouragement, affection, and obedience (2 Cor. 6:11–13).

Paul goes on to say that honor also includes financial care for preachers and teachers. The minister who provides spiritual food is to be treated at least as well as the ox that grinds grain. To the degree we are able, we need to ensure that pastors are fed (1 Tim. 5:18).

Paying pastors a living wage is necessary, but I suspect that Paul would want to do more than honor our pastors with pay. We should want to give them relief from their labour. It's not hard to give a pastor an extra week of vacation, or a couple weeks of study leave—which is not the same as vacation. If even that stretches the budget, permitting a half-dozen weeks per year where pastors are enabled to swap pulpits can give them extra time to catch up on work, or to do the praying and reading that they need for their own souls.

PRAY FOR YOUR PASTORS

An even better way to encourage our pastors is to pray for them. If we pause for a moment to think of all that pastors are called to be, we'll see just how much they need our prayers. Even if we skip over the five vices Paul says a minister must avoid, this is clear by the seven character traits they must display (Tit. 1:7–9b). Consider hospitality, the necessity to extend oneself because of the needs of others, and not because it is convenient to ourselves. Or consider what it takes to "love what is good"—not seeing how close he can get to sin without sinning, but how close he can get to heaven without dying. Pastors need our prayers to continue living this way.

But that's just the beginning. Pastors must also be self-controlled and upright, not swayed unjustly by large numbers or powerful personalities (does your church have any of those?). He is to be holy. Without personal holiness, everything else is a sham. And yet it's so easy for your pastor to care most about the duties that everyone sees and neglect the ones that only his Lord sees. Pray for them about this.

Finally, your pastor is to be devoted to the trustworthy message as it has been taught. The church needs men who love the gospel of the Triune God. There is a theological aspect to eldership. There are godly people who are still too ignorant about God's message in the Old Testament and the New Testament. They shouldn't be pastors until they grow in their knowledge of the truth, and then cling to that truth.

I said "finally," but of course we only glanced at a line or two in the New Testament, and there is so much more. If he is to be an under-shepherd of the Great Shepherd (Ps. 23 and 1 Pet. 5) and an intern under the great Physician (Mk 2:17), your pastor will need to feature largely in your prayers. If he is to live out the maxim of John the Baptist—that Christ must increase and he must decrease—then he will need your prayers (Jn 3:30). If he is to perform his good works not for your fleeting praise, but for our Father in heaven, then you know from hard experience just how much he will need your prayers (Mat. 6:1, 4, 6, 18).

CONCLUSION

Apart from paying them and praying for them, we can also encourage our pastors by heeding the message that they bring to us as ambassadors of Christ. Surely if God calls them to "preach the Word" (2 Tim. 4:2), then he is calling us to hear that Word. If he calls them to be leaders, then we must follow wherever the Word of God takes us.

As a visiting preacher once asked a congregation, speaking about their pastors, "Shall they beg mercy for you, and will you reject it? Shall they tender grace unto you, and you will resist it? Shall they open for you the door of life, and will you shut it against yourselves?" Or, to paraphrase his most important question, "Will Christ through them plead with you, and you refuse him?"[6] Heed your pastor's ministry. Nothing will encourage him more.

6   Edward Reynolds, *The Pastoral Office* (London, 1663), 46-47.

ABOUT THE AUTHOR

Chad Van Dixhoorn is associate minister of Cambridge Presbyterian Church and Grace Presbyterian Church in Vienna, Virginia, where he preaches weekly. He is also an Associate Professor of Church History for Reformed Theological Seminary's Washington D. C. campus.

Don't Muzzle the Ox

Ken Mbugua

Too often pastors neglect to disciple the saints on how to think about money with a biblical perspective. I trust that's an uncontroversial statement.

Pastor, do your people know how to answer difficult questions like these:

- How should Christians think about making money?
- Should they approach saving money differently than non-Christians?
- What principles come into play as they spend and invest money?
- How can they receive money as a blessing? How can they beware that money is also sometimes a curse?
- How can believers worship God through financial self-denial? How can they worship God by enjoying what God has given them?

If faithful Christians who attend church week after week remain in the dark about the answers to questions like these, it shouldn't surprise us that many churches don't know how and why they should pay their pastor. In this brief article, I will discuss three unbiblical approaches I've seen to paying pastors.

WHAT IF I WANT TO SERVE VOCATIONALLY IN THE MINISTRY WITHOUT TAKING A SALARY?

As a paid minister of God's Word, I feel some level of awkwardness surrounding this topic. After all, there's at least one place in Scripture where Paul explains why he and Barnabas did *not* draw a salary from their labor. But awkwardness was not on his list of reasons.

It's possible that there is a good reason for refusing to take a salary from a church that can pay you. But it's unlikely that your situation qualifies. When you find yourself ignoring clear commands like 1 Timothy 5:18 and holding on to exceptions like Paul not taking a salary for his ministry work in Corinth, you need to have a compelling reason.

If the duties assigned to a pastor don't make him leave his current vocation, then it's permissible not to pay a salary. The principle here is simple: how much time does it take to do his work well? However, when we make "tent making" the model for how all pastors should provide for themselves and their families, we deny the church the privilege of having a pastor fully set apart for the work of the ministry. He will have a divided mind and calendar, despite his best intentions.

I understand why the "tent making" model seems attractive, and some reasons are more noble and persuasive than others. For example, in some cases, "tent making"
could enable the gospel to advance in hostile places. But in other cases, I suspect this arrangement is one way the enemy keeps our churches weak.

We must search our hearts for the impulse that tells us to choose the path that keeps us from losing our identity in the marketplace. We must root our sinful desires that overly prize the respect of the world. If the church, especially in the area of preaching, needs a pastor to give up his vocation for the sake of the church, then so be it. May many qualified men flock to such a noble opportunity. We shouldn't hide behind "tent making" as *the* biblical model for *every* pastor. We are far too sinful not to suspect impure motives for breaking from the norms of Scripture.

The Bible teaches that a pastor's work is noble work (1 Corinthians 9:7), and when done vocationally it deserves remuneration (1 Timothy 5:17)—just like all honest work. These verses, especially 1 Corinthians 9:14, show us that it's right and biblical to think of such renumeration as a *salary*, not merely some kind of benevolent support. After all, Paul compares pastoral work to various "secular" vocations that would have been familiar to his audience. And then he concludes, "The Lord commanded that those who proclaim the gospel should get their living by the gospel" (1 Corinthians 9:14).

So, am I saying that one cannot have a day job in the marketplace and lead the church as a pastor who regularly preaches? Not necessarily. But I *am* asking you to be sensitive to the danger of cultivating an unhealthy culture of not paying your pastor. That culture in both the immediate future and in the long run will harm the church and its mission. Even if you don't need the salary because of inherited wealth or money made elsewhere, consider the example you're setting for how the church should relate to your successor. You're both weakening its generosity muscles now, and you are tempting them to look down on your successor for asking for an income. Better to receive that income now and enjoy the privilege of quietly giving it away.

WHAT ABOUT THE NEED TO DIFFERENTIATE BETWEEN THE

PROSPERITY GOSPEL AND THE TRUE GOSPEL?

Paul and Peter both warn about the love of money in the pastorate, referring to this in a King James' tongue as a desire for "filthy lucre" (Titus 1:11; 1 Peter 5:2). Our contemporary English versions use the phrase "shameful gain" (ESV) or "dishonest gain" (NIV) to translate the phrase. The warning for pastors here is that they should flee from and fight against the love of money. Poverty never disqualified a man from his post.

There are false teachers who "have hearts trained in greed" (2 Peter 2:14). These are the prosperity preachers who haven't heeded Scripture's warning. They love money, and so they have made the relationship between a pastor and his pay confusing to some.

So a minister of God's Word is free to refuse a salary if receiving renumeration would undermine gospel work in his specific ministry context. This was Paul's motivation to refuse pay among the Corinthians (1 Cor. 9:12-18).

That said, the places where the prosperity gospel runs rampant need both proper biblical teaching *and* healthy examples of how churches can care for their pastors financially. Christians need to see that money can empower the pastor to serve his church, and not merely to elevate him and his lifestyle above the congregation's— or, worse, to turn the church away from Christ and toward the false gods of worldliness, materialism, and mammon.

WHAT ABOUT MISSIONARIES WHO WORK FOR FREE?

Missionaries, who are supported by churches overseas, sometimes offer "free" counseling, preaching, teaching, and leadership to churches. In many global contexts, this free labor fosters complacency in indigenous churches. It makes it more plausible for Christians not to pay their pastors. In the most extreme cases, missionaries promote a hyper-spiritual view of money that results in the local pastors being grossly underpaid or not paid at all—even those who work full-time.

Sadly, it's not rare to see national pastors laboring in the ministry with limited or no pay while their wives and children languish in squalor. All the while, they're elevated as "models of faith" by traveling missionaries who themselves enjoy ample support from their home country. Now the pastors might be models of faith, but it's not to the credit of the churches they serve or the missionaries that lead them.

CONCLUSION

The matter of paying your pastor isn't a cultural issue; it's a biblical mandate. And it must be handled as such.

The Great Commission has in many cases been hindered by our neglect of this topic. God's Word languishes in the pulpit because churches have been taught to invest in buildings and projects, not men who have given themselves to the ministry of the Word. We have erroneously and even sinfully called the men to choose between disobeying the call to provide their own families (1 Tim 6:8) and the call to go for the sake of his name. While God might call pastors and missionaries to endure financial hardship for the sake of the advance of the gospel, no church is asked to make it their official policy.

ABOUT THE AUTHOR

Ken Mbugua is a pastor of Emmanuel Baptist Church in Nairobi, Kenya.

Maintain a Good Relationship with Christians from Other Churches

Jonathan Worsley

"Dare to discover Forbidden Island! Join a team of fearless adventurers on a do-or-die mission to capture sacred treasures from the ruins of this perilous paradise. Your team will have to work together and make some pulse-pounding manoeu-vres [around the board], as the island will sink beneath every step! Race to collect the treasures and make a triumphant escape before you are swallowed into the watery abyss!"

I read the box lid with skepticism. *"Join a team?"* *"Work together?"* This was a far cry from the dog-eat-dog board games of Monopoly and Risk I'd grown up with. Nevertheless, Forbidden Island has become a firm family favorite. Believe it or not, three somewhat competitive children (and one very competitive Dad) sit around the kitchen table and work together discussing strategies for capturing treasure and escaping an imaginary flooding island before our little counters sink.

What's the key to victory? Bizarrely, in this particular board game, it's all about players maintaining good relationships with other players. If The Engineer doesn't cooperate with The Explorer, we lose. If The Messenger refuses to give The Navigator their treasure cards, it means defeat for all. If The Pilot declines to rescue The Diver, game over.

Sadly, when it comes to real life, it can be tempting for many Christians (conceivably those of us who love our own local church most of all) to live like we're playing Monopoly or Risk. When it comes to other local churches, we think about *competition*. I want the most money, the most territory, the most treasures, the most people—for *our church*, of course. If relationships with other Christian players outside our own local church suffer, so be it. We want our church to win.

Some churches, sadly, cultivate this kind of philosophy. But many don't. It's our natural bent, after all.

When it comes to the Christian life, when it comes to how members of different gospel-preaching churches ought to relate to one another, we need to change our

strategy. We need to remember we're playing Forbidden Island—not Risk or Monopoly.

THE WHY

Here are a few reasons why.

1. Good relationships with other Christians occur because we're on the same team.

We should work hard to maintain good relationships with Christians from other churches because ultimately, we're on the same team. The common goal in this real-life game is not our personal glory but God's. Our opponents are the world, the flesh, and the devil (Ephesians 2:2–3). We fight for victory over these fierce powers, not for victory over brothers and sisters from different churches. Christians, therefore, strive to be a united team. And not only in their own local church, but as the church universal. For the church is one, as God is one. Christ saw the importance of this one team mindset and prayed that you and I might have it: "I do not ask for these only, but also for those who will believe in me through their word, that they may all be one, just as you, Father, are in me, and I in you" (John 17:20–21).

Practically, if we are Christians in a large city-center church and a gospel-preaching church plant sets up around the corner, we shouldn't scowl and draw our treasure cards close to our chest. Likewise, if we belong to the fledgling church plant, we should see resource-abundant Christians up the road as allies in a victory march, not as other players who could potentially scupper our chances of "winning." God's people rejoice when new players join. As Stephen Witmer helpfully writes, "In Psalm 48 we see God blessing his spectacular city, Mount Zion, the wonder of the whole world— and the villages and towns of Judah aren't jealous. Instead, they're jubilant, rejoicing along with the city. In the end, neither the city nor the country is ultimate: instead, it's God who gets the glory."[7]

2. Good relationships with other Christians help us capture more treasure.

In Forbidden Island, each player ascertains a certain skill at the start of the game. Some players can

7 Stephen Witmer, A Big Gospel In Small Places, p. 163

move around the board more rapidly; they often get the glory of capturing the most treasure. Other players keep the island from flooding. The Messenger has the very humble power of sharing his or her resource cards with others! To get as many treasures as possible, every player must use their own talents for the whole—even if that means some players collect none.

The same is true when it comes to real-life gospel success. The opportunity to unearth very real treasure—namely, unbelievers coming to Christ and Christians growing to be more like Christ—is often set in motion by recognizing our own aptitude, limitations, and location on the board.

One Christmas, when pastoring in London, I recalled that another local church had a plethora of gifted musicians. Last minute, I asked if they could help us put on an evangelistic carol service. They happily agreed (indeed, even their pastor played!) and the gospel was proclaimed. A few weeks later, a short-term mission team I knew was staying in London. I realized they couldn't serve our church as we were too far away, but I knew of an opportunity to serve another needy church. Good relationships with other Christians allowed more treasure to be gleaned.

3. Good relationships with other Christians help us shore up our island.

Christian success isn't only about collecting gospel treasure, but also about building up the church (Ephesians 4:11–16), and therefore keeping weary believers from going under. The very best way to keep Christians afloat is to foster deep relationships within local churches. By joining a certain church, we give certain pastors and certain Christians permission to support us amid the rising floodwaters of temptation, worldliness, and false doctrine.

But sometimes, we need other Christians from other churches to graciously and patiently counsel us. We especially need this if we're discontent or discouraged about something that's happening inside our own church. We often need people who are not personally absorbed in what we're facing to see it clearly. This is not to minimize the work of the local church in the pastoral situation. Indeed, I've often found that my best friends outside my church have supported me in such a way that has turned me back to my local church with empathy, compassion, and resilient commitment. Such shoring up can only happen if we work hard to maintain good relationships with Christians from other churches.

4. Good relationships with other Christians remind us our time is short.

There's a final characteristic of Forbidden Island which parallels the Christian life: time is short. In real life, we only get so many moves to capture sacred treasures from the ruins of this perilous paradise. The sands of time are sinking. As a result, Christians must work together locally and quickly. If we spend all our time squabbling over resource cards and planning others' next moves, then we'll lose. We should look at the clock as we strategize together for the sake of the lost and the immature. Sometimes we will plant the seed, and it won't germinate at our church. Sometimes we will faithfully water the plant, only for it to flower elsewhere. The fleetingness of our days here should make us care a little less.

THE HOW

With all this is in mind, how can we maintain good relationships with other Christians from other churches? Here are a few tips.

1. Spend time with other Christians from other churches.

When I pastored in London, once a month I'd go out with a Christian neighbor who was firmly committed to a large Anglican church in the center of London. On a personal level I'd really enjoy it. But spending time with him also reminded me that the Kingdom of God was bigger than my own church. And as he told me all the wonderful things that his church was able to resource, my pride and jealousy were revealed, which consequently helped me to fight them.

2. Encourage your pastor to spend time with pastors from other local churches.

Deep relationships take time. Don't sigh if you see your pastor out for lunch with his local pastor buddies, and think "Why isn't he in his study or at the hospital?" Amid all the laughter, he's hopefully fostering a trust and a unity, which in turn will benefit him, you, and most of all the whole church.

3. Speak well of other churches.

When we mention other churches in passing, there's the temptation to define them only by their faults. "Do you mean the dancing-in-the-aisles megachurch? Or the stuffy little one where they only let you in with a suit?"

Amazingly, Paul addressed the church at Corinth as "the church of God, those sanctified in Christ, who are not lacking in any gift" (1 Corinthians 1:2, 7) not "the proud, disorderly, sexually licentious Greeks who sue one other and get drunk at the Lord's Supper." In the same way, we should work hard to define other churches by their virtues and their standing in Christ. Speak well of those whom you will share eternity with.

4. Pray for other churches.

As we have opportunity, we should pray for all Christians, even those who might attend churches that we have some reservations about. At my current church, we pray for any church in our city that preaches the gospel. We pray for such churches by name in our pastoral prayers in our main weekly gathering. Every week, our small group Bible study notes have a section with names of other local churches to pray for.

5. Give to other local churches.

Again, the primary church we should give to is our own. We have the responsibility and joy to contribute generously and regularly to the ministry we glean the most from. Nevertheless, there may be opportunities to support other churches either directly, or through the encouragement of our church leaders. I remember my former church supporting the work of another in our city. I had some real questions about the robustness of their ecclesiology and their discipleship philosophy. But ultimately, they were moving into an area with no gospel witness. I wouldn't have made some of the moves they made, but I came to see that they were searching for treasure that I would never be able to exhume. We gave to them, and we rejoiced to hear of their labors for Christ.

CONCLUSION

We must work together on this sinking island as fearless adventurers on a do-or-die mission. We must play the game in front of us. We must play as best we see fit with the opportunities and skills graciously given. And we must play cooperatively, lest we become an island unto ourselves.

ABOUT THE AUTHOR

Jonathan Worsley is the pastor of Kew Baptist Church in the United Kingdom.

Be a Good Witness in the Community

Marwan Aboul-Zelof

I n my walk with Christ, I often know a truth before I really understand its significance. Similarly, I often know the things that Scripture says I should be doing, but I often struggle with *how* to do them. I imagine I'm not alone.

We all know Jesus' words in the Sermon on the Mount: "Let your light shine before others, so that they may see your good works and give glory to your Father in heaven" (Matt. 5:16, CSB). But many of us get stuck on *how* to shine our lights. Should I post more on social media? Should I serve at a local homeless shelter? Should I talk to my neighbors more?

As believers, we must apply the message of the cross to all of life. We must understand that the gospel has implications that are meant to bear fruit in and through our lives. The gospel compels and empowers us toward generosity, justice, brotherly love, and many other things! And it's this fruit that's a shining testimony of who Jesus is to our community.

THREE WAYS TO BE A GOOD WITNESS

Be Present

I run the risk of being redundant with this first point, but we can't be a good witness in our community if we're not in the community. We must be present.

You don't need to come up with a new hobby or cause for you to engage with your community. The joy and beauty of being a new creation in this world is that God will use you as he's created you. Your affinities and experiences, empowered by the Holy Spirit, make you perfectly qualified to be a good witness. Whether you're single or married, old or young, an extrovert or an introvert—God will use you to display his diverse family.

Our model for faithful presence in our communities is Jesus. "The Word became flesh and dwelt among us" (John 1:14, CSB). He is our example of how to walk with different kinds of people. And as we do, we trust that our Lord will give us opportunities to display his goodness and love.

Be Faithful

Whether you're committing yourself to a cause in the neighborhood, joining a community sports league, or are a regular patron at a café, you have the opportunity to reflect the faithfulness of God.

God's faithfulness is displayed through his unwavering commitment to his people. He has proven over and over again that he is worthy of our trust. And so, as his people, we are able to display varying degrees of this commitment and trust in our community interactions. Our presence and faithfulness lay a foundation for friendships and opportunities to be built.

Our dedication reflects the faithfulness of God, but so does our faithfulness to biblical convictions. The fact that we can care about and enjoy the same things as our non-Christian neighbors (*in the world*) without being conformed by sinful ways of living or thinking (*not of the world*) shows our neighbors the transformative effects of the gospel. It also dispels misconceptions they may have about Christians and Christianity.

Be Together

When Jesus gave the "new command" to love one another (John 13), he immediately said that this *one-another love* would show the world that we're his disciples. They will know we are Christians not by our wisdom or our strength, but by our love for God and for one another.

So how can you be a good witness in the community? Be together with Christians in the community. Swarm the world with goodwill. When we think of being a good witness, we should do so with other believers in mind so that our witness might be amplified.

CONCLUSION

In everything, let's be prayerful and intentional. Let's recognize that God doesn't need us to accomplish his purposes, yet he has given us the privilege to join in his work.

ABOUT THE AUTHOR

Marwan Aboul-Zelof is the planting pastor of City Bible Church in Beirut, Lebanon.

Evangelize the Lost

Eric Bancroft

Have you ever been driving home, only to get there and realize that you don't remember how you got there? I certainly have. You knew there were turns, stoplights, and stop signs, but you didn't remember them. You were on autopilot. You've gone home so many times, you've familiarized yourself with it so much, and you know the people there so well that you don't even think about it anymore. It might even be difficult giving people directions because you don't even remember the names of the streets or which landmarks are at which intersections. You just know how to get there.

This is what it is like for many Christians with their Bibles, in their churches, and among other Christians. No directions or explanations necessary. Everyone knows what to do and where to go. The preacher says, "Turn to Matthew," and no one thinks to look around them for a guy named Matthew. The Christians say to each other, "I really enjoyed the fellowship we had last night," and no one thinks it's a name of a Norwegian dish. They just know.

But this isn't true for those who didn't grow up in church and have never chatted with friends about heart idols, besetting sins, and preaching the gospel to themselves.

Here's the question I'm interested in: how do these two worlds intersect? How should we interact with our non-Christian friends, co-workers, and classmates around us in order that they might hear and believe in the gospel?

Here are five lessons to remember:

1. BE FRIENDLY.

There are plenty of times for one-and-done conversations with strangers about the gospel, but most evangelism opportunities are sitting in front of you on a regular, if not daily, basis. They're the people across from your cubicle (or in your Zoom meeting). They're the people you work out with or buy coffee from. They have histories of the life they've lived and hopes for a life they want to live.

For many of us, the initial challenge is not making disciples, it's making friends.

So take interest in people. Observe their life, ask about their weekend, learn about their relationships, and listen to their stories. Jesus talked to people. In between pronouncing curses on cities, challenging Pharisees on their logical fallacies, and restoring peace and order to a town by casting out demons, he talked to people. And their answers became conversational bridges to discuss eternal matters.

I'm not advocating for extroverted personality training. I'm putting some street clothes on Matthew 7:12, "So whatever you wish that others would do to you, do also to them, for this is the Law and the Prophets." I'm encouraging you to learn about people and find ways to love them and serve them as one who lives for the reputation of Christ, not yourself.

2. KEEP THE GOSPEL IN VIEW.

Have you ever told someone a story about something that happened to you and halfway through they interrupt and say that something similar happened to them? The problem is that after hearing their runaway story for a few minutes, you realize that it's totally unrelated to yours. This is quite common in conversations about the Bible with non-Christians. We try to head somewhere but they take the conversation elsewhere. Whether it's past bad experiences with "the church," beliefs about meditation, or the power of positive thinking, people bring up all kinds of topics once you start talking about Christ.

It's good to keep a good conversational roadmap in front of you as you think about your desired destination. The initial goal is friendly interaction. The intermediate goal is meaningful conversation. The ultimate goal is making disciples of Jesus. This can help us assess where we are in our interactions with others. Anything might come up: politics, reasonable curfews for teenagers, the exact dimensions of heaven. But through it all, the goal is to steer the conversation back onto the road of gospel clarity and conviction.

As you seek to do this, don't neglect prayer. Don't forgot to appeal to other Christians to pray for you and the people you're trying to reach (Col. 4:3–4). You're engaging in more than conversational jujitsu. You're engaged in truth for the sake of the lost, while encountering all kinds of opposition along the way (Eph. 6:12).

3. INVITE THEM TO BE YOUR GUEST AT A GATHERING OF CHRISTIANS.

Do you remember the first time you met your spouse's parents? No doubt you were a little intimidated, especially if the relationship was still in its early stages.

This is how many non-Christians feel when we invite them to church right away. They understand that Christians usually gather in groups called "churches," but they're a little taken back by the whole prospect of maybe getting up earlier on a Sunday than they normally would. They wonder what outfit they should wear; they wonder how much singing or talking they will have to do. Meanwhile, others are suspicious of churches—some for good reasons, some not—and they're not eager to go back to one.

This is why you could look for a time and a place with a lower barricade for them to get over. Are you and some church members playing pick-up basketball at the park? Invite your friend to join. Are you going out for dinner and a movie with church friends? Invite your friend to join. Are you hosting a get-together at your apartment to watch a game? Be sure to invite your friend!

These gatherings would be full of meaningful interactions with other Christians. Plus, they get to see small but significant acts of love between other Christians (John 13:34–35). Perhaps they'll hear you mention that you've been praying for someone. Perhaps they'll see you encourage one another in conversation—or not lose your cool on the court! In short, you want your non-Christian friends to see Christian love reverberate in other people's lives. Let these gatherings serve as an appetizer before the entrée—when they see Christians gathered together as local churches worshipping the risen Savior.

4. ASK THEM TO READ THROUGH ONE OF THE GOSPELS WITH YOU.

Many non-Christians, even those who grew up in churches, have actually never read the Bible. Yet they often have all kinds of opinions about God, Jesus, Christians, and truth. So ask your friend to read one of the accounts of Jesus' life and ministry for themselves and talk about it with you. Challenge them to get to know the Jesus of the Bible; challenge them to reject their incomplete or inaccurate representations of Jesus. I think you will be surprised at who says yes to this.

One great resource I recommend to you is David Helm's *One to One Bible Reading*. Helm's book offers different reading plans and strategies for this kind of Bible reading. It includes an eight-meeting plan through the Gospel of Mark, complete with questions for the reader to ask in each section. It will move the conversation and personal reflections toward gospel clarity.

5. KEEP THE BIGGER PICTURE IN MIND.

When people asked us what we wanted to be when we grew up, most of us probably didn't say we wanted to be farmers. And yet that's exactly what we are. Sure, you might be compensated for your time working at a bank, a convenience store, or a school, but that's not all you do. You're also called to the agricultural pursuit of planting the seeds of the gospel in people's lives. Whether it's a stranger on the Metro, a childhood friend who still lives in your neighborhood, or a new hire at your company, you are called to make disciples.

Let me encourage you to remember that success in evangelism doesn't depend on your skill, personality, or immeasurable Bible knowledge (Mark 4:26–27). It's the Spirit of God who uses the Word of God as told by the people of God—and all of this is done for the glory of God. Furthermore, no strategy, no list of tips, or no different reading plans will convince some people that the gospel is good. We're reminded that "the message the word of the cross is folly to those who are perishing." But the verse does go on to say, "but to us who are being saved it is the power of God" (1 Cor. 1:18).

Do you remember what happened in the Garden of Eden after Adam disobeyed? God pursued him. He went after him. He didn't wait for Adam to come to him. God has been doing that with sinners ever since. Let's do the same thing and remember "how beautiful are the feet of those who preach the good news!" (Rom. 10:15).

ABOUT THE AUTHOR

Eric Bancroft is the pastor of Grace Church, a new church in Miami, Florida.